GW01396247

Whine
& Dine

*Let us eat and drink; for tomorrow
we shall die.*
Isaiah, XVIII: 13

Whine & Dine

A TONGUE-IN-CHEEK GUIDE

Lesley & Cris de Boos

JARROLD

Other titles in the Humour Series available from
Jarrold Colour Publications:

Vicar's World by Patrick Forbes and Bill Ritson
Westminster Exposed by Ian Collins
Racey Bits by Mark Siggers and Chris Williams

Whine and Dine

ISBN 0-7117-0352-3
First published in Great Britain, 1988
Copyright © Lesley and Cris de Boos, 1988

Designed and produced by
Parke Sutton Limited, 8 Thorpe Road, Norwich NR1 1RY
for Jarrold Colour Publications, Barrack Street, Norwich NR3 1TR

Printed in England by
The Eastern Press Ltd., Reading

All rights reserved. No part of this publication may be reproduced, stored in a
retrieval system or transmitted in any form or by any means, electronic,
mechanical, photocopying, recording or otherwise, without the prior permission
of the publishers.

Illustrations by Chris and Jo Riddell on page 5 reproduced with their kind permission

About the authors

Lesley de Boos

Born in 1943 in London, having come down from Lincolnshire for the event, she was brought up in Norfolk and trained as a beautician and masseuse before setting up in business alongside her father, a physiotherapist. A friend asked her to help one New Year with a party he was giving, and it was such a success that her fame spread.

In 1975 she met Cris, an Australian, and decided that it would be such a good deed to adopt a poor stray Aussie that she let him marry her. They opened a restaurant in 1980 in a small Norfolk village and ran that for seven years, doing outside catering as well. It finally became too much to cope with both the restaurant and the catering, and so the restaurant had to go – the only recorded example of a restaurant closing because it was too busy.

She has a passion for cats, and is moderately fond of her husband.

Crispin de Boos

Born in 1947 in Sydney, Australia, he trained as an accountant before coming to England for six months in 1974. He married Lesley in 1978 so he could stay here – the original six months having expired. He worked for five years for a large accountancy firm in London handling receiverships and liquidations scattered throughout the country, and it was during the course of one of these that he met Lesley. He felt that Britain, having exported much of its talent during the transportation era, needed a man of his vision and experience and consequently decided to stay on and try to civilise the natives – in Norfolk a difficult and thankless task.

He ran the restaurant with Lesley, she doing all the cooking and he doing the front of house. It is a remarkable tribute to Lesley's talent that customers came in their droves in spite of him.

He is passionately fond of his wife, and moderately fond of cats.

Introduction

One must wonder how, after the invention of fire, cooking came about. It is probable that some animal fell into the ashes, a passing Neanderthal pulled the carcass out, burnt his fingers, licked them, liked the taste and immediately opened the first takeaway. It would have had to be takeaway as he could only follow the fires around to find anything else that had fallen in.

Since then man has been wandering the earth in an effort to find food and drink worthy of his efforts, and it's often been a frustrating search. The triumphs of finding a perfect *boeuf en croute* or a properly underdone vegetable have been offset by the opening of the newest, biggest, ugliest McSaunders Chickenburger outlet.

However, perseverance has paid off and now in this country we have thousands of restaurants, some of which even manage to serve good food.

There are also thousands of people who give dinner parties, having devoured the wisdom of all the glossy magazines given over to food and drink. The newspapers all have columns about where to dine and what to cook, and there's a plethora of television personalities extolling their particular modes of eating. No doubt we will soon be getting columns about where to get the most competitive loan to finance the next Dinner Out in London.

Health food and ethnic restaurants abound, and folk are now beginning to take seriously those once-great stalwarts of the boozer, the Indian and Chinese. In a different category are the health food restaurants. How curious it is that they seem to attract the most sickly and miserable looking people – it is as if all that healthy living has destroyed totally the capacity for laughter and enjoyment.

In Britain we do not as yet fully appreciate the European idea of casual dining and open air eating. Admittedly the weather is against us, but there is a growing awareness here of eating for relaxation and pleasure. With *nouvelle cuisine* on the way out, meals are becoming fun again rather than the serious business into which dining had developed.

This book is for entertainment, and is written 'tongue in cheek' – instruction is secondary, though we have included tips and some recipes that we hope will make your cooking and entertaining easier. There are a lot of our idiosyncrasies and eccentricities reflected – which is as it should be. The likes and dislikes are personal too, though they have been refined and collected through a lot of first-hand experience and sampling.

There are dedications – to 'the girls who come and play'. Many of the tales and comments come from them. And to Jonny, who first had the patience to let Lesley try her hand at cooking.

A **Adam's Ale**

Adam's Ale   'Madam, I'm Adam.'

'I perceive you're not Eve.'

Adam drank like a fish − nothing but water passed his lips − and 'Adam's ale' is, of course, water. The poor man had nothing else with which to quench his thirst. The Scottish, to be different, call it 'Adam's wine'.

Though essential for life, water's worth isn't always appreciated. At the opening of a Western Australian water scheme in 1902, to serve desert gold-mining towns, Sir George Reid remarked, 'Never have I seen so much enthusiasm for water − and so little of it drunk.'

To many people water's fine . . . if diluted with a little whisky.

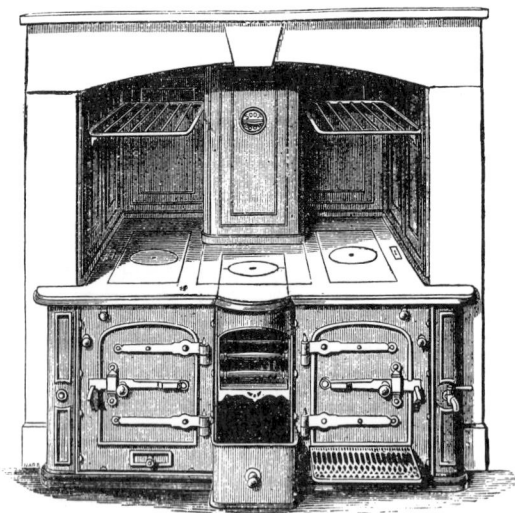

Aga   Wonderful invention for keeping large country kitchens warm and cosy, and producing hearty casseroles after a day's huntin', shootin' and fishin'. Adored by household pets, it is every cookie girl and caterer's nightmare. The words '. . . of course we've got an Aga' produce instant panic.

Invariably none of the ovens will be of the correct heat for whatever it is you're cooking, and with a houseful of guests and the central heating going full blast there will be no hot water at all.

Just when the guests reach cheese and port, the Aga will have reached the temperature you required four hours earlier.

Alcohol **A**

A la Carte   Literally, 'according to the sheet of paper' – a list of restaurant dishes which can be specially prepared on request, and so are more expensive than the *table d'hote* selection

> Keep teabags in a tightly-sealed container. They pick up other flavours easily.

Airline Food   This is a contradiction in terms. Airline food is the airborne version of what you get at a fast food chain.

Travel first class and you get real plates – not necessarily real food, mind, just real plates.

Best bet is to go vegetarian while you're airborne: for some reason the non-meat dishes are always best by far.

Hospitality: the virtue which induces us to feed and lodge certain persons who are not in need of food and lodging.
Ambrose Bierce

Alcohol   Every cook's lifesaver, alcohol has been around for millions of years. Under the right climatic conditions most moistened vegetable matter will spontaneously produce alcohol.

Perhaps the ancient riddle of why the dinosaurs disappeared may be put down to over-indulgence in the then prevalent rain forests.

It is probable that wine and beer, being products of natural fermentation, were accidental discoveries. There have been many reports of animals showing signs of intoxication – elephants ingesting overripe fruit which ferments in their large stomachs, and blind drunk monkeys staggering near pools of fermenting fruit dropped from trees. It is a nice thought that wine was probably discovered like this.

The word alcohol is from the Arabic *Al-kohl,* which means powdered antimony. This was used as an eye cosmetic, introduced in ancient Egyptian days, and was derived by a primitive form of distillation and refining.

In its less wasteful form, alcohol is called a stimulant, though it is in fact a depressant. It is not warming except psychologically – so much for the winter nip to keep the cold out. It does not improve sexual activity, but it does make the preamble more enjoyable.

A al dente

A well-known senior politician was known to be a heavy drinker. At a diplomatic function, as the orchestra struck up, he felt that as the senior British minister present he should start the dancing. Spying a colourful robed figure he said, 'Beautiful lady in scarlet, will you do me the honour of waltzing with me?'

'Certainly not!' was the sharp response. 'In the first place you are drunk; in the second this is not a waltz but the Venezuelan National Anthem; and thirdly I am not a beautiful lady in scarlet. I am, in fact, the Papal Nuncio.'

Fresh Fish

Do not gut fish or take the heads off before freezing. Wrap them in foil and freeze them, as far as possible, just as they came out of the river or sea.

al dente   Not a member of the Cosa Nostra, but meaning something cooked so it's still firm when bitten (Italian: literally 'to the tooth').

Not something generally understood by the English — they like to boil their vegetables to death, at which point they taste like dishwater.

Try undercooking carrots, broccoli, courgettes so they are still crisp. Chinese leaves lightly stir-fried are delicious.

Go on, be adventurous . . .

Allspice   The common name for the myrtle seed, this is a delicate, fragrant spice
with a taste of cinnamon, nutmeg and cloves. Good with game and
patés, or as a pickling spice. Also a tasty alternative to nutmeg with
milk puddings.

Madam, I have been looking for a
person who disliked gravy all my
life: let us swear eternal friendship.
Sydney Smith

American   Generally, the less said about America's contribution to international
Cooking   cuisine, the better. The home of hamburger and hot dog, cola drinks,
'Have a nice day' and large unattractive American tourists who top
the size of everything in England, America seems to be full of prepackaged food which is exported via franchises all over the world.

There are patches of excellent food scattered throughout – Creole
cookery drawn from French, African and American Indian roots, and
the Mexican influence in the far south and west are the two best
known – though these are much better in their native areas than
outside.

The 'hot dog' was stolen from the German frankfurter, the only
difference being that it's encased in a roll so it can be eaten outdoors.
It's normally smothered with a sauce of such potency that it
completely covers the original taste.

The American novelist James Fenimore Cooper wrote in the middle
of the last century:

The Americans are the grossest
feeders of any civilised nation
known ... The predominance of
grease in the American kitchen,
coupled with the habits of hearty
eating and the constant
expectoration, are the causes of
the diseases of the stomach which
are so common in America.

Even the great American dancer Isadora Duncan would rather have
lived 'in Russia on black bread and vodka than in the United States
at the best hotels. America knows nothing of food, love or art.'

A Angostura Bitters

Angostura Bitters
Originated in Venezuela in 1829, now made in Trinidad, and an essential ingredient of champagne cocktails and pink gins. Added to soups, casseroles and stewed fruits it imparts a lovely flavour.

Do be wary of asking for it in pubs, though. When asked for a lime, lemonade and bitters (a refreshing, long, non-alcoholic drink) in a northern pub, the barmaid looked blank.

'Don't you have any angostura bitters?' asked the customer. Back came the reply, 'No, dear – only Mansfield, Whitbread and Yorkshire.'

> *I have always maintained that there is nothing wrong with nursery food now that we are grown up and can have a glass of wine with it.*
> Elizabeth Ray

A Nice Glass of Warm White Wine
White wine should always be served cold. The people who make it want it served cold. The only difference of opinion might be the precise degree of coldness.

So why is it so common to go into hotels and pubs – which may proudly proclaim their collection of fine wines – and be served the cheapest example of the winemaker's art from a one and a half litre bottle which has been sitting around for weeks beside the microwave? It is not guaranteed to make an evening begin well.

A good publican will serve his beer at the correct temperature (mostly) – so why not his wines?

In a local bar, a glass of dry white wine was asked for. A glass of something that resembled old German socks was presented. Upon complaining, the drinker was told 'Wasn't it dry enough for you? It's Liebfraumilch.'

And some very good hotels and restaurants can be just as bad. It is, 'Sweet white or red – we don't do dry by the glass'.

The general rule to remember seems to be that the larger and more ornate the advertising extolling the excellence of the vinicultural wares, the worse the wines.

Glafs

> *At a dinner party one should eat*
> *wisely but not too well and talk*
> *well but not too wisely.*
> W. Somerset Maugham

Aperitif   The word *aperitif* means 'appetiser', but in this country it is usually applied to something liquid while 'appetiser' means something to nibble with it. A glass of sherry, or a gin and tonic and a stale potato crisp, is about the norm on this side of the Channel. But once out of England the word takes on a whole new meaning.

Throughout the Mediterranean countries the smallest pavement cafe offers a wide range of aniseed drinks – every country seems to have its own version – or a delicious vermouth.

In Spain the aperitif to drink would, of course, be sherry; in any wine-producing area a glass of the local product. All these drinks are stimulants to the appetite.

Originally an aperitif always contained something bitter, derived from roots of plants, in a strong alcoholic base (which probably did away with any benefit derived from the bitters).

Although the idea that one actually *needed* something to stimulate the appetite has probably disappeared, the pleasant habit of a drink before a meal lingers on (much to the relief of the disorganised hostess).

When deep-freezing garden produce, put polythene bags into plastic boxes before you fill them with peas, beans etc. then remove them when frozen. You will have square-shaped packets which will be easier to store.

Aphrodisiacs   As Polly Adler said, 'Too many cooks spoil the brothel.'

Throughout history food and sex have been closely linked, the temptations of the latter often enhanced by exotic concoctions of the former. Ovid describes in his *Metamorphoses* how he would send a slave to his mistress after a good dinner to acquaint her of the excited state of his loins and to ask if he could receive her at once.

The *Kama Sutra* – that first great book of the love arts – has many things to say about food and love, one of them being: 'If a man mixes rice with sparrows' eggs and, having boiled this in milk, adds to it ghee and honey and drinks as much of it as necessary, he will be able to enjoy innumerable women.'

A Aphrodisiacs

The most famous of all aphrodisiacs are rhinoceros horn and ginseng. There is no known reason why the rhinoceros horn has this reputation – perhaps its shape is to blame. Ginseng is apparently helpful to some degree. It's a Korean plant supposedly cooked in a silver kettle, and was drunk on its own or with rice wine.

The Egyptians thought that lettuce was an aphrodisiac – but the Greeks thought it induced sleep.

The mandrake root has a sinister reputation as a love philtre. Rachel was supposed to have eaten it before she attracted the attention of Jacob, and in Persia it was used to secure the love of one's husband.

Then there's the insect called Spanish Fly which, when dried, was very popular in its day. The drug it contains – cantharides – will induce priapism. But the danger is that the difference between the efficacious and the deadly amount is minute.

Asparagus is rich in potassium, phosphorus and calcium – good for maintaining a high energy level.

Caviare is 30 per cent protein and, because of its nature, has been considered particularly good. It also comes from the sea, and all fish and their by-products have been linked to the myth of Aphrodite, goddess of love, who was born from the foam of the sea. Spurred by her power, anything from the sea would, so to speak, give a lift to an affair.

Eels, garlic and lobsters all have their devotees, but oysters are perhaps the most renowned of aphrodisiac foods. Casanova called them 'a spur to the spirit and to love', and it has been said that eating a good oyster feels like angels copulating on your tongue.

The Chinese and Arabs held peaches in deep regard, and a 'peach-house' was once a common English slang term for a brothel. In English argo a 'peach' still describes a pretty or sexually-appealing girl.

Rabelais, Casanova, George Sand, Napoleon and Mme Pompadour all praised the aphrodisiac powers of truffles, though Casanova boasted that he really needed no artificial assistance. 'Women are my cuisine,' he was reported to say.

The list is endless – not only foods but drinks as well. It was discovered very early on that alcohol breaks down inhibitions and weakens the will to say 'No.' White wine contains phosphorus which is supposed to be an aphrodisiac, hence the reputation of champagne.

But, every would-be *bon vivant* should remember that moderation is necessary. According to the porter in *Macbeth,* drink provokes lechery: '...it provokes the desire but it takes away the performance. . .'

All animals are strictly dry,
They sinless live and swiftly die.
But sinful, ginfull rum-soaked men
Survive for three score years and ten.
And some of us – though mighty few
– Survive until we're 92.
Anon

Apicius   The only complete Roman cookery book to have survived is attributed to Marcus Gavius Apicius, who lived about the first century BC.

Apicius was a glutton who spent vast sums on feeding himself. When he realised that his fortune was dwindling and that he would probably not be able to afford to live in the manner to which he was accustomed, he poisoned himself.

His cookbook contains recipes such as stuffed wombs from sterile sows, dormice and camel, which sound pretty poisonous themselves.

Apple-pie   There are two schools of thought on the origin of this phrase, which
Order   means 'To put in prim and precise order'.

Some say that it comes literally from the way in which apples could be cored, neatly cut and methodically arranged when making a pie.

But more likely it is a corruption of the French for folded linen – *nappes pliées.*

A Apron

> *Woe to the cook whose sauce has no sting.*
> Chaucer

Apron　　　*Napperon* is the French word for a napkin (from *nappe*, meaning 'cloth').

Once in common usage the word changed from 'a napperon' to 'an apperon', and hence to an apron.

Archestratus　This Greek poet, born around 350 BC, was probably the first recorded gastronome. Attributed to him is the earliest cookbook in existence – a work in verse called *Gastronomy*. Unfortunately, only a few fragments of it have survived – like the following:

> *I write these precepts for immortal Greece that round a table delicately spread, three or four may sit in choice repast or five at the most. Who otherwise shall dine, are like a troop marauding for their prey.*

Artichoke　　The artichoke is a species of thistle. Boil the thing in salt and water; dip the ends of the leaves in oil and vinegar or hollandaise sauce before eating. Then enjoy the really fine flavour of oil and vinegar or hollandaise. . .

The globe variety makes an ideal meal for slimmers – by the time they've boiled and pulled off all those outer leaves, dipped the base into a low-calorie sauce and sucked it hard they're exhausted, bored and no longer hungry.

On the other hand, a few tinned artichoke hearts quartered and mixed with diced avocado – and a vinaigrette dressing to which have been added horseradish, tarragon and whole grain mustard – is quite a different matter.

Ripen avocados quickly by putting them in a fruit bowl with ripe fruit.

Australia Fare

Over the last 20 years Australian cooking has grown up. The ubiquitous meat pie, once found in every hotel bar, has quietly been forgotten. Instead Australians are beginning to discover that an abundance of local ingredients can be used to create a cuisine which rivals that of any other country.

Seafood and shellfish especially are amongst the very best available anywhere, and Australians now tend to eat great delicacies like fresh lobster and Sydney Rock oysters as a matter of course. Gone are the days when you'd be served a cup of tea and told, 'If yer don't loik it sweet, don't stir it'.

And it's not only the local food that's improving. Thanks to the influx in recent years of immigrants of all nationalities, Australian cities can now boast some of the best international cuisine to be found anywhere in the world.

Would-be diners in the Glebe district of Sydney, for example, are faced with a choice of Vietnamese, Thai, Japanese, Chinese, Italian, French, Swiss, Greek or Lebanese food . . . all at an affordable price and all on one half-mile stretch of road. Choosing where to eat on a Friday night can become a time-consuming and contentious exercise.

Many Australian restaurants are unlicensed, so the customers bring their own bottle. This isn't because the restaurateurs are too mean to supply wine, but because the licensing costs can be quite prohibitive. The advantage is that you can at least be assured that (a) you will like what you're drinking, and (b) you can afford it.

By the way, in the local vernacular a hotel is a 'rubbidy' (rubbidy dub, three men in a tub) – get it?

Store unwashed strawberries in a colander in the refrigerator, so air can circulate around them – they keep longer.

Australian Wine

Wonderul stuff. The days of Kanga Rouge and Chateau Billabong are well and truly gone. The whites rival the best that France can offer and the reds stand head and shoulders above so many traditional types.

The first vines were planted in 1788 by Captain Arthur Phillip – Governor of the then penal colony of New South Wales – but it was not until 1816 that the first wine was made.

The Australians invented the bag-in-the-box wine, and on the whole put moderately drinkable liquid in the bladder-like containers. In England, bag-in-the-box wines are generally not even fit for cooking purposes.

Probably the most successful Australian whites come from the Chardonnay grape. Often oak-aged, they are full of fruit and take a little getting used to. The reds are hefty and very full-bodied – more like Burgundies than Clarets.

Australian wine labels are full of information – describing the grape type; how, when and where the wine was made; the best temperature at which to drink it; how long it will keep and all sorts of other exciting and interesting trivia. It's not every bottle you can read as well as drink.

Avocado

A decade ago this delicious fruit was the smart starter in restaurants and at dinner parties, and in 1979 South Africa exported 10,644 tons of them to us.

It contains no cholesterol, very little carbohydrate, lots of protein, vitamins, minerals and unsaturated fatty acids. An avocado will ripen quickly in a fruit bowl with other fruits, and is economically one of the best buys.

Eat the delicious flesh raw or lightly cooked; rub the skin over rough areas of the body – elbow, hands, heels; or grow a pretty indoor plant from the stone.

It's so versatile, you certainly get your money's worth!

Baked Beans The most boring thing that ever came out of a tin, yet generations of people who should know better seem to have been reared on them. Orange in colour and bland in taste, they are a triumph of advertising over sense.

Baker's Dozen The weight of bread, rolls etc. was very strictly regulated in the Middle Ages and any baker found underweighing his product would be severely punished. To put an extra item to each dozen was his protection against any accidental deficiency.

Bananas This delicious and nutritious fruit can be served in sweet or savoury dishes, raw or cooked – and can even be mixed with any vegetable oil to make a moisturising face-pack.

Fried in butter with a few almonds, a banana will turn a piece of grilled or fried fish into a party dish.

To make a super last-minute pud, fry bananas in butter and brown sugar with some orange juice – and add brandy at the last minute. If you really want to show off, set light to the brandy. With a dollop of whipped cream it won't taste at all of improvisation.

Lastly, of course, it is the essential ingredient of the now-famous banana and toffee pie (said to be Mrs Thatcher's favourite) – and so delicious it brings out the worst in people.

> ❝ *Tell me what you eat and I will tell you what you are.*
> Brillat-Savarin ❞

Bank Managers A necessary adjunct to everyone's life. Their general policy is to give you lots of money when you don't need it and take it away when you do!

In a well-respected restaurant a bank manager was overheard to say, 'I just like to come along occasionally to see what I own'.

Arsenic omelettes were unfortunately not on the menu.

B Banquets

Banquets   During the early Christian era there was little private dining. Meals were communal and the diners sat on long wooden benches – *bancos* – later corrupted to 'banquets'.

Prehistoric man pioneered banquets by slaughtering animals on the occasion of the two great events of his life – birth and death.

In ancient Egypt, the women took charge of organising banquets. The Egyptians were very careful in their cooking, for they believed the wrong choice and cooking of foods caused illness. Guests firstly washed their hands and feet in an anteroom on their arrival, and then took part in various games before the feast. When moving into the dining area they were bedecked with wreaths of flowers, drinks were served, prayers said and the meal begun. The guests sat on the floor and the dishes were placed near them.

Entertainment went on during these Egyptian meals, and it has been recorded that a coffin with an imitation skeleton was sometimes brought in so that guests could be stimulated to appreciate the more earthly pleasures of life.

The Assyrians celebrated the victories of their armies with banquets, some of them lasting for a week. The drinking vessels they used had no feet on them, so their contents had to be downed in one go.

Athenaeus reports on a Persian banquet, 'One thousand animals are slaughtered daily for the King's table: horses, camels, oxen, asses, deer and most of the smaller animals. Many birds are also consumed, such as Arabian ostriches, geese and cocks.'

In Greece, in addition to the banquets held on special occasions, citizens were required to eat a sacred meal together every day, within the *prytaneum* in the presence of the gods. To miss a single day would be to lose the favour of the gods. The men were selected by lot to attend and were severely punished if they did not. Those who sat at the sacred table were called *parasites* – a sacred title then. The rich drank wines from Vienna, Italy and Greece. The poor had beer and *hydromel* – herb and spice-flavoured honey, diluted with water.

The Romans were probably the most ostentatious of all. At one meal guests were served 600 ostrich brains, peas with grains of gold, and lentils with precious stones. Guests were required to bring their own napkins and changed into white robes and sandals on arrival. Musicians and dancers appeared, and sometimes gladiators performed.

Gaius Petronius, a favourite of Emperor Nero, was invited to a special banquet at Nero's palace. The meal was to be followed by a 'licentious entertainment' featuring a hundred naked virgins. Petronius refused the invitation thus – 'Tell the Emperor that one hundred naked virgins are not one hundred times as exciting as one naked virgin.'

Banquets – Persian style

Nine kings, five queens, sixteen presidents and approximately 500 other exceedingly elevated people were guests of the late Shah of Persia in 1971 when His Imperial Majesty gave a banquet to celebrate the 2,500th anniversary of the Persian Empire.

In opulent tents erected beside the ruins of the imperial city of Persepolis, they ate a princely meal prepared by 150 chefs flown to Iran from Maxim's of Paris.

The contents of some 25,000 bottles of wine were poured into magnificent crystal glasses (and then into Very Important Throats).

The food, served on priceless Limoges plates, included partridge with *foie gras* and truffle stuffing, quail's eggs, and sole stuffed with caviare. It is understood that these standards are not maintained today.

B **Barbecues**

Barbecues | The lazy cook's ideal way of eating because everyone wants to help. Rare? Medium? Well done? Forget it – it all comes burnt to a crisp.

Barbecuing originated in Haiti. As salt was scarce the natives invented their own method of preserving meat – they smoked it over an open fire on a grid called a *berbekot*. When the Spanish arrived, they liked the idea so much they adopted it and called the cooking device *barbacoa*. The word and the device were taken to North America and in time came to describe not only the cooking platform, but the whole manner of eating outdoors.

Barbecuing is for hot countries where eating *al fresco* is a pleasant pastime. It is not designed for countries where chefs have to stand outside in the rain over a fading fire in winter jackets, before bearing a burnt offering to guests seated – inside – at the table.

The Americans love barbecuing and spend a fortune on huge motorised spits – often on wheels – with built-in refrigerators, griddles, hotplates, and music centres. Somehow seems to take some of the fun out of it . . .

Basil | This herb gives one of the predominant flavours in Mediterranean cooking, is *the* herb to use with tomatoes, and is also essential for the production of Chartreuse.

Holy basil – *Ocimum Sanctum* – is a sacred herb to the Hindus, and in Egypt it is scattered over graves.

It is a delicate plant and should be grown on the windowsill in this country.

From an old English herbal:

> *Fair Basil desireth it may be hir lot*
> *To grow as a gilly flower trim in a*
> *pot,*
> *That Ladies and Gentils whom she*
> *doth serve*
> *May help hir as needeth life to*
> *preserve.*

Bay | Not properly-speaking a herb, but the leaf of the bay tree, *laurus nobilis*.

The bay leaf is one of the basic ingredients of a bouquet garni and is found in most recipes for casseroles and marinades. It is also used to impart flavour and to decorate patés.

Laurel leaves were also used in classical victory garlands and the wreath awarded for academic achievement – hence the term 'poet laureate'. University students who graduate are Bachelors, from the French *bachelier,* which in turn comes from the Latin *bacca laurens* – laurel and berries. At one time these scholars were not allowed to marry in case they were distracted from their academic careers. So all unmarried men came to be called 'bachelors'.

When cooking with beer use it warm. If chilled it loses most of its flavour

Beans

Though beans come in all sorts of shapes, sizes and colours they have one universally attributable trait – they are all stodge.

Beloved of vegetarians, the dictionary defines them as the seed pods of leguminous plants. In Greek they're *blammos,* in Sanskrit *fut,* Chinese *ga-pao,* and Old German *blatte.*

The Latin name, however, says it all – *detonatae.*

Beaujolais Nouveau

The sooner this unseemly dash to France to bring back the first bottle of their vinegary new season's wine is forgotten, the better. It does, however, give restaurants the opportunity to put on a special over-priced 'fun' evening where everyone can wear their berets and Bretons.

The French love this peculiar British habit as, for large sums of money, they sell stacks of what is often a very mediocre product. One good reason for ceasing this practice is that vineyards in the Beaujolais region will then be encouraged to allow their wines once more to develop and age and to produce good Beaujolais!

A cucumber should be well sliced and dressed with pepper and vinegar, and then thrown out as good for nothing.
Samuel Johnson.

Beer Money

This was an allowance of one penny a day paid to British soldiers and NCOs between 1800 and 1823, instead of an issue of beer. The term has moved into modern-day usage to denote spending money for re-freshment or pleasure.

Beeton,
Mrs Isabella

Mrs Beeton's *The Book of Household Management,* first published in 1861, is probably the most famous of all cookery books. It is a work on domestic economy and contains some 4,000 recipes.

In the preface to the first edition in 1861 she wrote, 'I must frankly own, that if I had known, beforehand, that this book would have cost me the labour which it has, I should never have been courageous enough to attempt it.'

Her book aimed to give 'an intelligent arrangement to every recipe, a list of ingredients, a plain statement of the mode of preparing each dish and a careful estimate of the cost, the number of people for whom it is sufficient, and the time when it is seasonable.' She did not really invent any recipes, and candidly acknowledged that most of her recipes came from readers of *The Englishwoman's Domestic Magazine.*

Two years after she died at the age of 28, her husband became an editor for Ward, Lock & Co but broke the terms of his contract. As partial recompense, he left the publishing firm the rights to some of his wife's books – a lucky break for them, as Mrs Beeton's cookery book has rarely been out of print since.

Biggest
Banquet,

The prize for the biggest banquet ever must surely go to the event organised by the President of France on 22 September, 1900. In a vast tent set up in the Rue de Rivoli in Paris, he entertained all the mayors of the towns and villages of the republic – 22,295 of them.

It was a great success. They feasted on:

Hors d'oeuvre
Fillet de boeuf en Bellevue
Pains de canetons de Rouen
Poularde de Bresse rotie
Ballottine de faison Saint-Hubert
Salade Potel · Glace succès Condé
Desserts

In other words:

Hors d'oeuvre · Filleted beef
Duck paté · Roast chicken · Boned pheasant
Salad · Ice cream · Fruit

Birdseye,   It is this gentleman we have to thank for the overwhelming range of
Clarence   frozen products available in every supermarket and shop.

A scientist and inventor from New York, he went to Canada as a fur trader in 1912 and saw how the local people froze their food for the winter. Back in New York he experimented with rapid refrigeration methods, freezing food between two refrigerated metal plates.

The first Birds Eye commercial pack was put on the market in 1929 and caused a revolution in food selling. In appearance and taste, products were almost as good as the fresh original, and were often more palatable and nutritious than canned food. What a pity Birdseye's original standards have now melted away.

Incidentally, the following was once seen on a children's menu – 'Birds Eye Cod Pieces and Chips'.

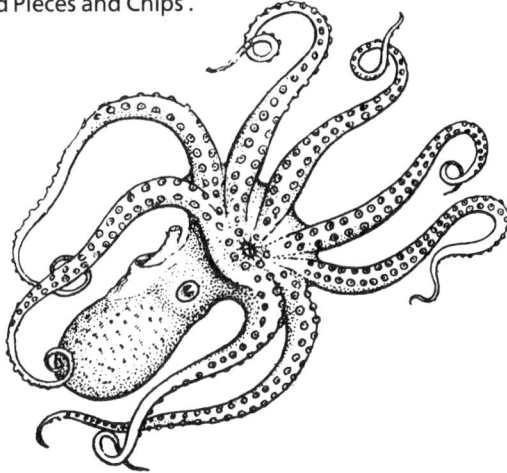

Bits and   The Mediterranean countries are far more imaginative than we are
Pieces   in their bits and pieces to nibble with drinks – some bars and tavernas serve nothing else.

The Spanish *tapas* bars are famous, and in Greece there are many establishments, often Turkish in origin, which open only a few hours each evening to serve *ouzo* and *meze.*

The idea of serving these titbits is to stimulate the appetite (and the thirst), though when they're fairly substantial and delicious they sometimes replace a first course.

Just look back to sunny holidays and think of delicious plates of juicy tomato, cucumber, olive and goat cheese, and the elegant array of *crudités* with garlicky mayonnaise.

The chewy pieces of octopus and morsels of salty fish may take a bit of getting used to. But they beat a salted peanut or a Twiglet any day!

Black Forest Gateau

The dessert equivalent of chips. Many restaurants assume that it is the only pud most people have heard of. Yet it has surely become the most maligned of all gateaux over the last decade.

Ideally it is a luscious layered chocolate cake soaked in kirsch-flavoured syrup on a crisp biscuit base, the layers sandwiched with whipped cream and black cherries.

Unfortunately, it is all too often a ready-made cake sandwiched with a tin of pie-filling and an oversweetened cream substitute. It has the consistency of cardboard, the taste of soap and is to be found on many sweet trolleys – usually an indication of a restaurant to be avoided.

> *I never see any home cooking.*
> *All I get is fancy stuff.*
> **Duke of Edinburgh**

Bloody Mary

The Bloody Mary was invented by a Frenchman for Americans in Harvey's New York Bar in Paris, during the prohibition era.

As a long drink for cold lunchtimes it is hard to beat; it is also a hangover curative, a meal in itself and a marvellous pick-me-up.

To ice cubes and a large measure of vodka in a tall glass add (to taste) salt, pepper, lemon juice, angostura bitters, Worcestershire sauce, tabasco and brown sugar. Top up with tomato juice and stir with a stick of celery.

There are many imitations. Bloody Maria is a tequila version, and Bloody Virgin is non-alcoholic. The Bullshot is made with condensed consommé instead of tomato juice, and is an excellent corpse-reviver.

Knife

Blunted Knives

It was as a result of an incident at a banquet given by the celebrated 17th-century French statesman, Cardinal Richelieu, that the refinement of blunt table knives came about.

He noticed one of his noble guests cleaning his teeth with the point of his knife, and was so disgusted he ordered his staff to blunt all such implements.

From this aristocratic beginning the habit spread and has never been abandoned.

**Boiled
Cockatoo**

From an old Australian cookbook:

> *The proper way to cook a cockatoo is to put the bird and an axehead into a billy. Boil them until the axehead is soft. The cockatoo is then ready to eat.*

Bottles

It used to be a lot more confusing than it now is to work out what bottle-size to buy – particularly when purchasing wines. Legislation is now being introduced to ensure that all wine is sold in 75 cl. bottles, and the old 70 cl. size is being phased out. Spirits should be in 75 cl. bottles, with the exception of brandy which comes in bottles of 68.5 cl.

The following variations are also available:

Split – a quarter-bottle, used for champagne and for the rot-gut they sell on aeroplanes.

Half-bottle – useful size for solo drinking, though wine growers tend not to put decent wines in half-bottles. Too expensive, they say.

Magnum – two-bottle size. Great wines are often put down in magnums, as they age and develop more slowly in larger bottles.

Marie Jeanne – an unusual three-bottle size, sometimes called a tregnum.

Jeroboam – four bottles of champagne or five bottles of Bordeaux.

Rehoboam – six bottles.

Imperial or Methuselah – eight bottles.

Salmanazar – twelve bottles.

Balthazar – sixteen bottles.

Nebuchadnezzar – twenty bottles.

B Brandy

> *What is sauce for the goose may be sauce for the gander, but it is not necessarily sauce for the chicken, the duck, the turkey or the guinea hen.*
> Alice B. Toklas

Brandy   As defined by the Ministry of Food, brandy is 'the distillate of the fermented juice of fresh grapes without the admixture of any other spirits'. A very boring definition of an eminently drinkable product.

The term 'brandy' covers all spirits distilled from wine – from Cognac and Armagnac at the top end to grape brandy and fruit brandy at the bottom end.

Cognac was probably discovered by accident, the wine producers of Charante having boiled down their poor-quality wine to make it easier to transport. This idea spread and the powerful end product became known as brandy from either the Dutch *brandewyn* or the German *branntwein* – both meaning 'burnt wine'.

The English took to it as there was no native spirit until gin came along, and by the 18th century brandy was the tipple of the aristocratic and middle classes. Brandy smuggling went on even during the wars, and in some parts of England was the sole money-earning industry.

Ambrose Bierce in his *Enlarged Devil's Dictionary* was particularly vicious about it:

> *BRANDY. n. A cordial composed of one part thunder-and-lightening, one part remorse, two parts bloody murder, one part death-hell unto the grave, two parts clarified Satan and four parts holy Moses! Brandy is said, by Emerson to be the drink of heroes. I certainly should not advise others to tackle it.*

Brandy or Gin?

An alderman of London, Sir William Cooper, was a guest at a banquet held by the London Clothworkers Company. He imbibed freely of his hosts' brandy and when he arrived home he dropped down dead.

Lady Cooper accused the Clothworkers of having killed her husband with their noxious brandy, and when she died she left a sum of money to the company with which to buy gin as an alternative.

This choice of brandy or gin is still offered at the Clothworkers' feasts with the words, 'Do you dine with Alderman or Lady Cooper?'

Wrap fresh herbs in aluminium foil and freeze until needed.

Bread

The most basic of foods has been around since the Stone Age, and unleavened bread (containing no yeast) was included in the diets of the early Egyptians, Hebrews and Chinese.

Contrary to popular belief, the nutritional value of commercial brown and white bread differs very little as extra nutrients are added to white flour.

There is, however, a considerable difference between the flavour and texture of commercial and homemade bread, and perhaps everyone should have a try – just once – at making their own.

It actually isn't the time-consuming operation that people imagine. After all, you don't have to watch it rise. And there really is a little bit of magic about the way that soggy little bowl of dough turns into beautiful, fragrant loaves.

Whether you choose the super-quick Grant loaf or a more conventional method, your efforts will undoubtedly be rewarded by cries of 'Ooh – homemade bread!' and you can feel justifiably virtuous and earth-motherish.

Just one word of warning. Perhaps it might be better not to attempt the Greek peasant bread made with a leavening of basil – it takes four days to make!

Breakfast

The first meal of the day – the one at which the night's fast is broken. During the Middle Ages the majority of the common people rose at dawn and broke their fast with watery ale, curd cheese and bread or pottage made from rye, barley or oats. It was not until the Victorian era that bacon and eggs appeared on the breakfast table, but it was just one of many meat, ham, egg and fish dishes served at the large breakfast to be eaten by people who would be out all day.

B Brillat-Savarin

Breakfast should pave the way for the rest of the day, but Winston Churchill said, 'My wife and I tried to breakfast together, but we had to stop or our marriage would have been wrecked.' Hotel breakfasts are summed up by Ogden Nash:'... and you stagger down to break your fast, greasy bacon and lacquered eggs, and coffee composed of frigid dregs.'

E. M. Foster put into perspective the English Country Home cry of 'Porridge or prunes, sir?':

> *It is an epitome – not indeed of*
> *English food but of the forces*
> *which drag it into the dirt. It voices*
> *the true spirit of gastronomic*
> *joylessness. Porridge fills the*
> *Englishman up, prunes clear*
> *him out ...*

Conversation at breakfast is a difficult thing. Far too often the cereals eaten are so snapping, crackling and popping that you can't hear what is being said. The only warning you get that the rest of the breakfast is ready are the smoke signals from the toaster which is incinerating your toast. Take heart, though, from Oscar Wilde. 'In England,' he said, 'people actually try to be brilliant at breakfast. That is so dreadful of them. Only dull people are brilliant at breakfast.'

Continentals either give you coffee and a bread roll or – like the Dutch – cereals, cheese, cold meats, sausages, boiled eggs, yoghurt, fruit and coffee.

Australians used to eat steak and eggs for breakfast, but the ultimate is the Kentucky breakfast – a bottle of rye whisky, a steak and a dog. The dog is there to eat the steak.

Brillat -   Jean-Anthelme Brillat-Savarin, born 1755 in Belley, near the Swiss
Savarin   border, was perhaps the best-known gastronome of the 18th century.

He was a great advocate and judge and published many tracts and pamphlets on law and legal matters, but he is most famous for his gastronomic work *La Physiologie du Gout*, published just before his death in 1826.

He had been preparing the work for years, travelling all over France to taste the regional specialities, and he was the first to acknowledge just how much French cuisine owed to the influence of other countries.

'French cookery,' he wrote, 'has annexed dishes of foreign extraction such as curry and the roast beef of England; condiments such as caviar and soya; drinks such as punch. Coffee has come into general use, as a food in the morning and after dinner as a tonic and exhilarating drink.'

In his *Physiologie du Gout* he also established the rules of harmonious dining. His rules included that the dining room be luxuriously lit, clean and warm; the men 'witty without pretensions and the women charming without being too coquettish; the choice of dishes be exquisite, but restrained in number, and the wines of the finest quality. The speed of eating (should) be moderate . . . the coffee be scalding hot', and 'the guests should be held by the pleasure of the company, and stirred by the hope that the evening will not pass without some further entertainment.'

A lady once enquired of Brillat-Savarin whether he preferred Burgundy or Claret. He replied: 'That, madame, is a question that I take so much pleasure in investigating that I postpone from week to week the pronouncement of a verdict.'

B **Bucks Fizz**

Bucks Fizz   The name comes from the smart *Bucks Club* in 1920s London, which first served this up in England. It is a good party drink, made with freshly squeezed orange juice and good dry sparkling wine in 50/50 proportions.

Strawberry Woman

Open-freeze raspberries, strawberries and blackcurrants on trays – then put them into bags. They will stay separate so you can easily remove however many you need.

Cadbury,   In 1824 a young Quaker by the name of John Cadbury opened a shop
John   in Birmingham mainly to sell tea and coffee. But he also advertised 'cocoa nibs, prepared by himself, an article affording a most nutritious beverage for breakfast.'

This proved so popular that he began experimenting by grinding cocoa beans and began selling his powdered cocoa and chocolate under his own name.

A small factory was set up and demand grew to such an extent that ultimately his sons George and Richard moved the factory out of town and established for the workers a model village called Bournville.

Calories   For a perfectly calorie-free drink, take a mixture of water and club soda – and feel extremely virtuous.

For something a little tastier, a glass of cider vinegar at 14 calories is acceptable. A glass of wine contains 80 calories for dry white, 74 for red and a mere 73 for champagne. Spirits have 55 calories per 1 oz. measure, excluding the mixer.

On the food side cucumber, raw lettuce, rhubarb, cooked cabbage and celery will tot up between 13 and 16 calories per 4 oz. portion. For a blowout, when that extra sustenance is needed, raw celery and radish add up to a colossal 17 calories per portion. (At the other end of the scale butters, salad oils and lard contain about 900 calories per 4 oz.).

If one needs to lose some of the calories digested after consuming much of the above, it is suggested that one goes to a cocktail party and stands around (expending 20 calories), walks slowly towards an attractive target (115 calories), makes love (150 calories) and then bicycles home (on average 400 calories).

All the above, by the way, are per hour with the obvious exception being per act.

> *All the best cooking is simple. There is really nothing new in it. I have 4000 cookbooks dating back to 1503, and everything that is in* nouvelle cuisine *was there 200 years ago.*
> Anton Mosimann

Canapé Literally, a crustless piece of bread cut into rectangular shapes. But canapés shouldn't be made from bread from a three-day-old loaf, nor should they be made so far in advance that the soggy cheese cracker and cold toast variety results.

The overall sheen of aspic often seen on canapés is always ominous and usually signifies that they have been around for some time.

Get away from all the breads and pastry usually associated with canapés. Use crunchy vegetables as receptacles for tasty fillings. Tiny cherry tomatoes scooped out and filled with horseradish mayonnaise are good, and celery lends itself to many fillings – cream cheese and walnut, blue cheese or a highly flavoured thick mayonnaise.

If bread is used it must be fresh, well buttered and not too crumbly. Pumpernickel or rye cut into tiny rounds are firm and delicious. Pipe with cream cheese and decorate with mock caviare, red and black, and you have a very up-market morsel.

Pinwheel sandwiches always look attractive and are not at all difficult (they will freeze too). To make them, remove all the crusts from a day-old sandwich loaf. Slice it lengthwise and roll each slice hard with a rolling pin. Butter the slices well and spread with different fillings. Then roll up the slices and leave them in the refrigerator for a few hours – slice them thinly when needed.

C Caraway

These same slices of day-old rolled bread can also be used to make little layered sandwiches — very impressive and all done ahead of time. Simply make a large four-layered sandwich with different-coloured fillings, leave it in the refrigerator as with pinwheels, then slice it into tiny squares and arrange on a long dish. Looks as though the host has slaved all day.

Hot canapés are always greeted with great enthusiasm, and the possibilities are endless. If you have a deep fat fryer, make a batch of choux pastry in the usual way and stir in some tiny dice of gruyère or cheddar cheese. Deep-fry small teaspoons of the mixture until it puffs up and turns golden brown. Sprinkle with cayenne for a little more 'bite'. Deliciously different . . .

A few plaice fillets will make a lot of savoury nibbles. Cut into tiny strips with scissors, dip in flour, egg and breadcrumbs and spread on trays to freeze. Deep-fry from frozen, and serve with tartare sauce (homemade, of course). Much cheaper than scampi.

Much easier, obviously, to open a few packets of crisps and peanuts. But the satisfaction of seeing happy guests, who've enjoyed something better than just another boring cocktail party, will be ample reward.

> **Looks can be deceiving; it's eating that's believing.**
> James Thurber

Caraway   A rather old-fashioned spice, in the form of seeds, used in cakes and in a Dutch cheese.

It is also the base of kummel, a liqueur, which tastes like alcoholic gripe water. The resemblance isn't surprising, as caraway is known to have a carminative effect (i.e. it expels wind!).

Cardamom   This spice, which belongs to the ginger family, is widely used in Indian cookery and in pickling. A few seeds chewed after a meal are supposed to sweeten the breath.

Catering   At some time in most people's lives there comes an occasion, large or small, for which they cannot, or do not wish to, cook for themselves. This means rounding up friends who enjoy cooking — or, for a really large function, calling on caterers.

Bringing in the professionals will instantly produce feelings of terrible guilt — ought one to do it oneself; what will friends think; isn't it an awful extravagance? But once the party has been enjoyed and the kitchen looks as though nothing has happened in it, all such feelings disappear, along with the washing up.

Of course, there are good and bad caterers, but good ones should leave the host with happy guests, no mess and a satisfied feeling of having given a good party.

A caterer can be the answer to all problems of entertaining. They know where to get china, tablecloths, flowers, marquees and, above all, they know how much food and wine is needed.

It is awfully easy to overlook the fact that a hundred people don't eat ten times the amount that ten people do . . .

> *Old people shouldn't eat health*
> *foods. They need all the*
> *preservatives they can get.*
> **Robert Orben**

Caviare   'Caviare comes from the virgin sturgeon' as the old song has it, and caviare has been a delicacy since Roman days. During the Middle Ages in England only royalty could eat caviare. Sturgeon – like porpoises and whales – were classed as Royal Fish and if caught were forfeited to the Crown.

Few people in England can afford caviare so we have had to learn to lump it: the lump fish gives a passable imitation of caviare for decoration.

> **He:**
> *Tell me, my dear, how did you find*
> *the caviare?*
> **She:**
> *Oh, quite by accident, when I lifted*
> *the quail egg.*
> **Caption from a French cartoon**

Whale

Champagne   Disraeli was the guest of honour at a public dinner. The kitchens being some way from the banqueting hall, most of the food was stone cold by the time it reached the table. Sipping his champagne after the meal he was heard to murmur, 'Thank God! I have at last got something warm.'

The British drink more champagne than anyone else, yet seem to understand it least of all. Champagne is a region of France, and during the 16th and 17th centuries the still red and white wines of

C Champagne

Champagne had competed with those of Burgundy. During the reign of Louis XIV (1643-1713) Burgundy won, and it is said that this loss of prestige of the Champagne wines inspired Dom Perignon to invent the champagne we drink today.

Sparkling wine had been around for years, but it was unappreciated and rather volatile. What Dom Perignon did was to adapt cork as a special type of stopper and have the bottles strengthened. Corks were tied on with twine – the wire came much later. These adaptations succeeded and sparkling champagne was adopted by and drunk in the court of Louis XV.

Don't be deluded into thinking all champagnes are the same. Much better to serve a good *Méthode Champenoise* sparkler than a poor champagne – and there are lots of poor champagnes about, 'wedding' champagne being a particular villain.

This wine should not be looked upon as an expensive luxury – it's an affordable necessity of life, and needs to be treated kindly and drunk with respect.

George Bernard Shaw was once seen drinking a glass and was chided by his companions as he had held that he was a teetotaller. To which he replied, 'I am a beer teetotaller, not a champagne teetotaller.'

Always lay wine on its side so the cork is kept wet.

**Champagne
Cocktail**

The only sensible drink before a party.

Take one sugar cube and rub it on an orange; place in the bottom of a glass, add a few drop of angostura bitters and a little brandy – too much brandy and you completely ruin the cocktail. Fill with good sparkling wine (or champagne, if you're feeling flush).
Top-ups are made by putting the sugar cubes, angostura and brandy in a jug, pouring a little of the mixture into empty glasses and filling with the wine.

**Champagne
Glass**

The saucer-shaped champagne glass is said to have been modelled on the bosom of Madame de Pompadour (a lovely thought). However, this flat glass is impractical, easily spillable and dissipates the bubbles.

Without the bubbles, why drink champagne? They may give you hiccups, but that is a small price to pay.

A tall flute is the best glass from which to drink this particular beverage.

> *Let us have wine and women,*
> *mirth and laughter, sermons and*
> *soda – water the day after.*
> Lord Byron

Chartreuse

Of all the great liqueurs it is only Chartreuse that is still made by the monks. The recipe was given to the Carthusian Order in 1605, though nothing was done with it until 1764 when it was developed for public consumption.

Invented in 1838, Yellow Chartreuse is weaker and sweeter than the green – 40 per cent alcohol compared with 55 per cent for the green.

There are two variations to the basic liqueur: Chartreuse Cardinal – one-third green to two-thirds yellow; and Episcopal – two-thirds green to one-third yellow.

> *Gazing at the typewriter in*
> *moments of desperation I console*
> *myself with three thoughts.*
> *Alcohol at six, dinner at eight, and*
> *to be immortal you've got to be dead.*
> Gyles Brandreth

C Chateaubriand

Chateau-briand

Francois Rene, Vicomte de Chateaubriand (1768-1848) was a French writer and noble whose most famous work was the *Génie du Christianisme,* a vindication of the Church of Rome.

After the book's publication in 1802, so the story goes, he was dining in a Paris restaurant when the owner created a new dish in his guest's honour. A thick piece of beef was grilled between two other slices of meat, and when the outer pieces were almost charcoal the centre – a truly tender and luscious steak – was presented to Chateaubriand. A tribute to Chateaubriand's Christian fervour, the three pieces of meat were supposed to represent the two thieves crucified either side of Christ, symbolised by the rare centre piece.

A more prosaic explanation is that Montramil, Chateaubriand's chef, invented the dish while he was working in London, to be served at diplomatic dinners. To please his master he called it Beefsteak Chateaubriand.

Cheese

Clifton Fadiman described cheese as milk's leap toward immortality. It is certainly the latest 'speciality' craze to join real ale, coffee and tea and is now chosen with as much care as the wine for a special party.

But as G. K. Chesterton said, 'Poets have been mysteriously silent on the subject of cheese.'

Children C

Chervil   This is another herb which was brought from the Mediterranean, probably by the Romans, and which has enjoyed new popularity since it became a favourite garnish in *nouvelle cuisine*. With a flavour similar to parsley but milder, it was used far more in cookery in the 15th and 16th centuries than it is today.

It has the reputation for being a restorative for the elderly and those whose memory or brain is failing, and because of this earned the name *cerefolium* or 'brain-leaf'.

If you need white wine for a recipe and have none, use a glass of water with one tablespoon white vinegar and two tablespoons of sugar.

Children   When asked how he liked children, W. C. Fields replied, 'Boiled or fried'.

Similarly restaurateurs, when asked if children are welcome in their establishment, have been known to reply, 'Only if they fit in the oven'.

It is unfortunate, but understandable, that most British restaurants – other than fast-food chains, who make their living from selling junk food to children – have this attitude towards the very young.

But on the Continent children eat with their parents from a very early age, even being given watered-down wine rather than fizzy orange or other tooth-rotting liquids. This way they grow up with the experience of dining out and of the correct behaviour that goes with it.

In this country children are often fed at different times and on different food, so a visit to a restaurant can be a nerve-racking experience. If there are no fish fingers, baked beans and plates of chips, boredom sets in and tantrums follow to the embarrassment of all.

Occasionally the behaviour of parents rivals that of their children. Take the case of the mother who calmly told her offspring, 'Take off your wellingtons if you want to climb over the furniture.'

Robert Benchley said, 'There are two classes of travel – first class and with children'. The same sentiment can all too often be applied to eating with them, though sometimes adults get their own back.

The following advertisement recently appeared in a Bournemouth paper:

Labrador Cross, free to good family
home, 10 months, trained, lovely
nature, obedient, eats
anything – loves children.

C Chinese Cooking

Buy Great Eels

Chinese Cooking

Ignore take-away Chinese food, and remember that to the Chinese cooking is an artistic activity in which the preparation and presentation of the ingredients are as important a part of the meal as the food itself. Though rice is the staple diet, because of China's large population nothing was ever discarded as being inedible.

In 628 the Emperor served fried locusts to show his people that a plague of these insects was not a sign of displeasure from the gods, but an evil that could be put to use. Rats were called 'domestic deer' and snakes 'eels of the thicket', and were cooked and eaten regularly.

In the West most Chinese restaurants adapt the menus to suit the foreign palate and many dishes, such as chop suey, have never seen China at all.

> *One cannot think well, love well, sleep well if one has not dined well.*
> **Virginia Woolf**

Chocolate

'Chocolate' comes from two Aztec words – *xococ* (bitter) and *atl* (water).

As a drink, chocolate arrived in Europe before coffee did, imported by the Spanish from conquered South America. There, Emperor Montezuma and his court were reputed to drink 50 large jars of it a day. Sugar being unknown, it was flavoured with vanilla and drunk cold.

Beyond the court, there was a much more practical application – the beans of the cocoa tree were used as coins . . . showing that once money really did grow on trees.

Chocolate is made from the dried, roasted and polished 'nibs' or almonds of the cocoa bean. These are crushed, and when the resulting liquor is partly defatted, it solidifies into a hard block — bitter chocolate. This is generally used for cooking. Milk chocolate has powdered or condensed milk added with sugar, and is flavoured with vanilla, almond, cinnamon etc.

According to legend, Columbus was the first European to see cocoa, but the specimens he took back to Spain were considered of no value. So it was in France that chocolate first became a fashionable drink. Its first recorded use in England was at Oxford in 1650. Seven years later a Frenchman opened a cocoa house in Bishopsgate, London, and chocolate houses became very fashionable, each having a literary, political or gambling clientele. Whites, the gaming house in St. James's, began as a chocolate house.

When chocolate was first sold for eating is uncertain, though an 1842 price list of Cadbury products does show one kind of eating chocolate.

Chocolate was a cause of some controversy when it first reached Europe. Some claimed it to be 'an inducement to love', Madame du Barry and Casanova amongst them, and in 1669 Marie de Savane 'Took too much chocolate, being pregnant . . . that she was brought to bed of a little boy who was black as the devil.'

Christmas Day 1870

Stuffed Donkey's Head
Elephant Consommé
Roast Camel à l'Anglaise
Jugged Kangaroo
Roast Ribs of Bear with Sauce Poivrade
Haunch of Wolf with Sauce Chevreuil
Truffled Antelope
Cats flanked by Rats

(Served at one of the most chic of Paris restaurants with exquisite wines on Christmas Day 1870 — the 99th day of the siege of Paris.)

Under siege from the Germans, the Parisians were facing starvation. Horsemeat was being sold as an under-the-counter delicacy, and householders were becoming adept at cooking their own starving pets.

The situation was so desperate that a Monsieur Deboos, a leading Paris butcher, even had the idea of buying up the Paris Zoo – as the animals were also starving. Reportedly 27,000 francs were paid for the zoo's prize elephants, Castor and Pollux, and trunk meat fetched 50 francs per pound.

A gourmet whose subject was natural history arranged a dinner that included dogs' liver brochettes and shredded loin of cat mayonnaise. Impromptu cookery books were rushed off the presses.

It was said that cats tasted like rabbit, poodles were finer flavoured and elephants were tough and oily.

Chutney   Originally from India, this strong sweet relish was called *chatni* in Hindustani. At the end of the 17th century the East India Company first shipped it to England, and adopted and adapted the name. As one enthusiastic admirer wrote:

> *All things chickeny and mutt'ny*
> *Taste better by far when served*
> *with chutney.*

Cinnamon   A sweet fragrant spice, surprisingly good with fish and baked ham. It is the bark of the cinnamon tree and the sticks are used to flavour casseroles and curries as well as to stir mugs of hot chocolate. Also very good with apple pies and mulled wine.

Cloudy   Whatever it's called, every country seems to have one of those
Spells   delicious aniseed-flavoured aperitifs so often associated by the British with lazy sunny holidays.

Ouzo in Greece, *raki* in Turkey, *pastis* in France and *arak* in the east – all go cloudy when water is added.

Their high alcohol content ensures that without the water the drinker is the one that goes cloudy.

Cloves These are the dried flowers of the clove tree, used whole or ground. Spicy and aromatic, they are used for pickling, flavouring, for decorating baked hams, and in cakes and apple pies.

In Elizabethan times cloves were used in pomanders, as they're considered to be a powerful antiseptic.

Keep meringues in the airing cupboard in polythene bags to keep them in perfect condition for several weeks.

Coffee Legend has it that thousands of years ago Arab shepherds noticed that sheep which had eaten berries from a certain bush became lively and excited and would stay awake all night. It didn't take long for the shepherds to experiment with those berries, and discover coffee.

Legend also has it that a Moslem priest was led to the discovery of the coffee bush by the Prophet in order to keep the priest awake at his devotions.

In any event, coffee became widely used amongst devout Moslems who looked upon it as a divine gift brought by an angel from heaven to the faithful.

The use of coffee spread, and the first recorded coffee house in Europe was established in 1551 in Constantinople. The Grand Vizier feared that such places would become hotbeds of sedition, and ordered their closure. Owners who did not comply were beaten for their first offence, and upon the second were sewn into leather bags and thrown into the Bosphorous.

In England in the 17th century, coffee houses were known as 'penny universities' because the entrance fee was a penny, and men of every occupation and political affiliation met there to discuss the affairs of the day. Lloyds, the insurance house, began life as a 'penny university', and in *The Tatler* of 12 April 1709 Sir Richard Steele wrote: 'I date all gallantry from White's; all poetry from Wills; all foreign and domestic news from St. James's, and all learned articles from the Grecian.'

The coffee houses then began to come under attack from Puritans. The 'Women's Petition Against Coffee' of 1674 said that coffee led men to 'trifle away their time, scald their chops and spend their money, all for a little, base, black, thick, nasty, bitter, stinking, nauseous puddle water'.

C Cordon Bleu

Instant coffee was the invention of one Mr G. Washington, an English-man living in Guatemala. He noticed a fine powder on the spout of his silver coffee pot, which seemed to be a condensation of the coffee vapours. He experimented in 1906 with grinding beans, and in 1909 soluble coffee was first put on the market.

To the four basic methods of brewing ground coffee – boiling, steeping, percolating and filtering – may be added a fifth, beloved of some restaurants and hotels: reheating yesterday's leftovers. In many places, too, you get coffee totally swamped with milk – whether you want it or not.

Christopher Fry once remarked that 'Coffee in England is just toasted milk.'

Coffee will not cure drunkenness. If you pour mugs of coffee into someone who has had too much to drink, all you have is a wide-awake drunk.

> *The way to a man's heart is through his stomach.*
> **Fanny Fern**

Cordon Bleu   A cordon bleu was originally a knight of the French Order of the St Esprit (Holy Ghost), and so called because his insignia was suspended on a blue ribbon. The knights of the Order of St Esprit met together as a sort of club and were renowned for the excellence of their repasts. Anyone who had a superb meal would say, 'Bien, c'est un vrai repas de cordon bleu.'

Louis XV always maintained that only men could attain excellence as cooks. His mistress, Madame du Barry, disagreed and invited the King to a supper prepared by the best cuisinière in France. After the meal Louis wanted to know who the cook was and said he must have him in the royal household.

Madame du Barry produced the cook – a woman – and demanded a recompense worthy of both His Majesty and the cook, saying 'I cannot accept anything less than a cordon bleu.'

The King agreed, and so it was that the Cordon Bleu – the blue ribbon of the grand cross of the Order of the Holy Spirit, the highest chivalric order under the Bourbon kings – became the accolade of outstanding cooks.

If you need to make a lot of ice, make it in large plastic margarine boxes.

Coriander

At one time a spice in common use in this country, but now thought of mainly as a Middle Eastern or Indian flavouring. Coriander seeds have been found in a Bronze Age hut in Kent and are the first trace of an imported spice.

Although mainly used with meat dishes, coriander is wonderful with salmon and vegetables, especially cabbage and carrots.

Crepes Suzette

It is far from clear who should get the credit for creating this succulent little pancake. But one story is that it was first made for Edward VII, then Prince of Wales, by that prince of chefs, Escoffier.

When the new dish was presented to him, HRH asked what it was. It had as yet, he was told, no name. Escoffier asked for a suggestion, whereupon the Prince promptly named it after his dinner companion.

With his record of womanising, it could be that she was one of the few conquests whose name he would remember thereafter.

Whilst it is undeniably true that people love a surprise, it is equally true that they are seldom pleased to suddenly and without warning happen upon a series of prunes in what they took to be a normal loin of pork.
Fran Lebowitz

Cumin

A very pungent spice, used either ground or in seed form. Cumin's flavour is similar to caraway but stronger, and it features extensively in Mexican and Indian cookery. It goes well with curries and lamb or chicken dishes, and is very good with any dried beans.

C Curnonsky

Curnonsky Pseudonym of Frenchman Maurice Edmond Sailland, a renowned writer and gastronome who, more than anyone else, brought together the joys of tourism and eating.

As Curnonsky, he travelled extensively in Africa, and in China where the cuisine left an indelible imprint on his mind. He proclaimed it to be the best in the world, recording that 'France and China are the only two countries that have both cuisine and courtesy'.

Curnonsky embarked upon a 32-volume work called *La France Gastronomique* which covers most of French regional cookery from a tourist viewpoint, but only 28 were completed. In 1927 he was crowned 'Prince of Gastronomes' in a public referendum, and in 1928 founded the Academy of Gastronomes.

At the time of his death in 1956, over 60 restaurants in France always kept a table permanently reserved for him.

Custard

> *A detestable substance produced by a malevolent conspiracy of the hen, the cow and the cook.*
> **Ambrose Bierce**

Most schoolchildren would agree.

Daiquiri A proper daiquiri is made by shaking together white rum, fresh lime juice and grenadine syrup, which is then poured into a cocktail glass or over crushed ice. The daiquiri is making a comeback in the United States, and all sorts of mutations exist – strawberry or raspberry daiquiris, nutty-flavoured syrups replacing grenadine.

There is a doctor in New York who, after a hard day at the surgery, stops off at the same bar every evening to have one daiquiri, but made with almond essence. This routine is unvarying and the bartender knows exactly what his customer will have, and has it prepared for him at the right time.

One night the barman discovers he has no almond essence and in desperation uses hickory flavouring in the drink. The doctor takes a sip and says, 'This isn't an almond daiquiri, barman.'

'No.' says the barman. 'It's a hickory daiquiri, doc.'

Peel onions under running water so they do not irritate the eyes.

Dessert In early days, the dinner table was completely cleared at the end of the meal to make way for puddings. The French word for clearing is *desservier* and from this action of removing everything from the table came the word 'dessert'.

Diets Diets always begin tomorrow, and are only for those who are thick and tired of eating. And remember the advice of H.S. Leigh:

> **If you wish to grow thinner,**
> **diminish your dinner**
> **And take to light claret instead of**
> **pale ale;**
> **Look down with utter contempt**
> **upon butter**
> **And never touch bread till it's**
> **toasted or stale.**

Dill Usually thought of in connection with Scandinavian cooking, dill is very much the flavour of the month, due partly to the popularity of *gravad lax* (marinated raw salmon) in which it is used. It's also good with baby new potatoes, courgettes, and cucumber salad, and is, of course, an essential ingredient of dill pickle.

The name comes from the Norse word *dilla* meaning 'lull', and the herb is thought to be good for insomnia.

Called 'Meeting House seeds' by early American settlers, dill seeds were chewed at prayer meetings to relieve the monotony of boring sermons.

Dinner Companions When sitting at dinner parties, one has very little control over one's companions on either side. A story is told about the former American President, Calvin Coolidge, who was renowned for his reticence. At a dinner party the woman next to him coyly said, 'I have made a bet, Mr Coolidge, that I could get more than two words out of you.'

'You lose,' replied the President, and remained silent throughout the rest of the meal.

D **Dinner Parties**

A silent guest is very embarrassing. An over-attentive or demanding companion, however, can be even more trying.

At a dinner party in Victorian London, a 'society' lady found herself seated next to a French Count, and determined to monopolise his attention. Each time he tried to converse with others she would drop something on the floor, and of course the Count had to retrieve it for her.

Finally he'd had enough and, turning to the footman behind, said, 'Place my plates and cutlery on the floor. I shall finish my dinner there. It will be so much more convenient for the lady.'

> *What I love about cooking is that after a hard day, there is something comforting about the fact that if you melt butter and add flour and then hot stock* IT WILL GET THICK. *It's a sure thing! It's a sure thing in a world where nothing is sure; it has a mathematical certainty in a world where those of us who long for some kind of certainty are forced to settle for crossword puzzles.*
> Nora Ephron

Dinner Parties

Either loved or loathed. Hosts should remember that the guest is the most important person and that the idea is to make him/her as comfortable and as relaxed as possible.

The guest should never know that the chimney caught fire, the cat was sick on the only tablecloth and that the hostess is suffering from a rare disease that precludes even sniffing anything remotely resembling alcohol.

But while a guest can usually be relied on to relax and enjoy it all, with the family it's a different matter. They *have* to eat the food you dish up, and if they can complain they probably will.

If things get desperate, remember what happened to Helen Hayes. As she retired to the kitchen to put the finishing touches to the dinner preparations she warned her family, 'This is the first turkey I have ever cooked. If it isn't right, I don't want anybody to say a word. We'll just get up from the table, without comment, and go down to the hotel for dinner.'

She returned some ten minutes later to find the family seated expectantly at the dinner table – wearing their hats and coats ...

Double Entendres

A diner's guide to double meanings:

'I have traditional tastes' means 'I will not try anything new, ever'.

'I don't think I will have *that*' means either (a) 'I don't understand the menu'; or (b) 'That's far too expensive'; or (c) 'It's probably got garlic'.

'I don't think we'll have anything to drink' means either (a) 'We're not here to enjoy ourselves'; or (b) 'My husband drinks far too much anyway'.

'This place looks nice' means 'This place looks cheap'.

'Is it all right if the children have some of ours?' means 'The children will eat for nothing, and we'll probably ask for extra bread'.

'Can I have a half portion?' means 'I'm too mean to pay for a full meal.'

'My wife will have a taste of my starter/dessert/main course' means 'May we have two sets of cutlery?'

We just want something light – we're going out to dinner tonight' means 'We're going to take up a whole table at peak time for a cup of tea and one scone'.

'It all looks very nice but I won't have any' means 'It looks better than mine and I'm not bloody well going to try it'.

'It's too nice to cut into' means the same as above.

Drink

The first cup for thirst,
The second for pleasure,
The third for intemperance
And the rest for madness.
Anon

So declared Anacharsis, a philosopher of Scythia, an ancient state on the Black Sea, around 500 BC. Some things, clearly, don't change.

At a dinner party in Hollywood the American scriptwriter Herman Mankiewicz had too much to drink and threw up at the table – much to the horror of the other guests. Mankiewicz turned to his host and apologised, saying, 'It's all right, the white wine came up with the fish.'

D Drunk as a Lord

Drunk as a Lord *Brewers Dictionary of Phrase and Fable* records that, in the latter half of the 19th century, those who could afford to drink often as a matter of course drank to excess. Few dinners ended without the guests being hopelessly intoxicated.

As it was generally only the nobility who could afford to give such dinner parties the phrase 'Drunk as a lord' arose to describe the state of the host and his guests.

Duck Ducks were first domesticated by the Chinese 2500 years ago, but they were not introduced into Europe until the 16th century. About 80 AD, the Roman poet Martial declared in his famous *Epigrams*, 'Let a duck certainly be served up whole; but it is tasty only in the breast and neck; the rest return to the cook.'

Duck *à l'Orange* – a favourite of restaurants – will invariably be a frozen, ready-prepared meal, all bone and no meat, with the orange flavour a travesty. Boned and stuffed they are much better.

Duck Ham In France, duck breasts are cured in the same way as ham to make 'duck ham', which is then sliced very thinly like Parma ham.

> *Nature will castigate those who don't masticate.*
> **Robert Fletcher**

Dunmow Flitch In Dunmow, Essex, it was the custom that if a married couple could swear under oath to have lived for a year and a day in peace and tranquillity without a cross word passing between them, they were awarded a flitch – a side of bacon. In 1751 one winner cut the flitch into wafer thin slices and sold it among the 5000 spectators.

When Queen Victoria and Prince Albert were offered it a year and a day after their marriage it was, surprisingly, rejected.

**Edible
Dormice**

Everyone knows that gypsies eat hedgehogs. But what is perhaps not so widely known is that in France they still do as the Romans did and eat dormice.

The Romans would fatten them before a feast in special earthenware jars and feed them on acorns and nuts, which apparently gave the meat a nutty almond flavour. Their weight was recorded by the nobles' secretaries, as there was a certain amount of competition to produce the fattest dormouse.

Then they were stuffed with minced meat and pine kernels and served with a honey and poppy-seed sauce.

Frozen turkeys are juicier if defrosted in the refrigerator.

Eggs

Samuel Butler said, 'A hen is only an egg's way of making another egg', and where would we be without this fruit of the hen?

Eggs are, like yeast, an ingredient with that little bit of magic which can make soufflés rise, custards set and that runny concoction you add to butter in a hot pan turn into a featherlight omelette.

Light enough for invalids, but substantial enough for a main course, there is no meal at which you cannot eat them.

The Chinese have their '1,000-year-old' eggs – which is an 'eggsaggeration'. They are coated in a mixture of tea, ash, charcoal, lime and salt and packed in earth for a hundred days. Presumably they are then eaten.

There is a story told of a landlord who had the honour of serving King George II with an egg. He asked for one guinea in payment.
'It seems that eggs are rather scarce hereabout,' said the king.
'Oh, no sire,' replied the innkeeper. 'Not the eggs – the kings.'

> **Eggs of an hour, bread of a day, wine of a year, a friend of thirty years.**
> *Italian Proverb*

Eggs is Eggs

Not an expression relating to eggs, but probably mathematical in origin – as sure as X is X.

E Egyptian Cooking

> ## Part of the secret of success in life is to eat what you like and let the food fight it out inside.
> **Mark Twain**

**Egyptian
Cooking**

Egypt was conquered by the Arabs in the seventh century AD, and became – and stayed – Moslem. It was invaded by the Turks, by Napoleon and finally occupied by Britain in 1882. There has always been a large foreign population and all have made their mark on the cuisine.

The national dish is *ful medames* – brown beans steamed in salt water and served with crushed garlic, olive oil, lemon and hard-boiled eggs. *Meze* was brought to the Arab world by the Greeks and Turks, and pulses and rice are part of the staple diet. Vegetables are plentiful – especially okra and aubergines – and globe artichokes are a summer favourite.

Savoury pastries made with the light *filou* pastry and *falafel* (little balls of ground fried chickpeas) are sold on the street along with water and *soos,* a drink based on liquorice root. Patisserie is based on *filou,* including the delicious *baklava* with honey and nut stuffing and *ma'amoul,* tiny stuffed pastries.

The sheep is the only animal raised for meat: cattle are uneconomical and pork is forbidden. Spices are used extensively – saffron, cinamon, allspice and cumin seed.

Keep leftover raw onion in a screw-top jar in the refrigerator.

En croute

Literally 'in crust'. Often a croute or croustade would have been a hollowed-out loaf or broiche. Now it almost always signifies something in puff pastry, and it transforms the most simple ingredients into a dinner party dish. Try lamb chops, pork fillet, sausage meat or chicken breasts, and for special occasions, fillet steak or salmon.

Entrées

Not as the word implies the first course, but in a classic French menu the course which follows the fish. As very few of us still have a fish course every day it has come to mean the main course.

As he lay on his death bed Richard Melnes, the British writer, politician and *bon vivant* observed, 'My exit is the result of too many entrées.'

Etiquette **E**

Escoffier,   Kaiser William II said to Escoffier: 'I am the Emperor of Germany but
Auguste   you are the Emperor of Chefs'.

Born in 1847, Escoffier practised his art for 62 years until his retirement
in 1921, and in all cooking history there is no other example of such
a long professional career. He became chef at the new Savoy Hotel
in London in 1890 and eight years later took charge of the kitchens
at the Carlton Hotel, then one of the most famous in Europe.

His most valuable contribution to the culinary world was to make the
art of cooking respectable. When he started his career, chefs were
regarded as no more than inferior servants whose work in the kitchen
was degrading. He banned smoking and drinking in the kitchen and
ruled that chefs were not to be seen in dirty 'whites' by the public –
they were to change before going out.

Much of his skill lay in the simplicity of his style and his refusal to use
inferior ingredients. He tried to establish new modes of cooking by
getting away from the heavy sauces that were in vogue, and many
of the famous kitchens of the day were set up by him to his own very
exacting standards.

In 1893 he honoured the Australian singer, Dame Nellie Melba, by
creating the peach dish that bears her name. He was probably the first
chef to have a commercial association with a food manufacturer.
Many of his creations called for a popular mass-produced ingredient,
ham and anchovy essence, and he was paid handsomely for
recommendations of that particular brand.

The creations of his long career are recorded in two memorable works
– the *Guide Culinaire* written with the help of a colleague, Urbain
Dubois, and *Ma Cuisine,* which contained the best of his recipes. He
died in 1935.

> *In England there are sixty different
> religions and only one sauce.*
> **Voltaire**

Etiquette   Etiquette is a French word meaning 'label', from which is derived the
English word 'ticket'.

At formal functions an 'etiquette' would sometimes have been issued
to indicate the procedures to be followed, dress to be worn etc. From
this it came to mean a generally-accepted code of behaviour.

F Familiarity Breeds

Familiarity Breeds

When ordering a drink, never ask for 'the usual' unless you are positive that the barman knows what your 'usual' is.

Should he be in a bad mood, or think that you are just showing off, you may risk getting yesterday's slops in your glass – which you will have to drink as your 'usual'.

Conversely, a restaurateur should not presume to be over-friendly with his customers when they have unknown guests with them.

There is the tale of the restaurant-owner who welcomed a regular patron with 'It is so nice to see you again and to meet your son – he is just like you.'

To which came the frigid response; 'But he's not my son. He's my boyfriend.'

> **Better is a dinner of herbs where love is than a fatted ox and hatred with it.**
> *Proverbs, 15:17*

Farinaceous

All this word means is flour, and it generally describes all pasta – spaghetti, ravioli, macaroni, vermicelli – which comes as strips, tubes, hollows, stars, squares, spirals, shells and rings, and in a variety of colours. Irrespective of what they're called or how they are shaped, one thing is sure – they all taste much the same. It's the added sauces which make them enjoyable.

Ambrose Bierce defined macaroni in his *Devil's Dictionary* as 'an Italian food made in the form of a slender hollow tube. It consists of two parts – the tubing and the hole, the latter being the part that digests.'

Farmer, Mrs Fanny

The 'Mrs Beeton of America' was Fanny Farmer, and her *Boston Cooking School Cookbook* was first published in 1896.

She learned to cook at the Boston Cooking School and, after graduating, she took over the school and ran it from 1891 to 1902. She then opened Miss Farmer's School of Cooking to train housewives rather than cooking instructors.

She was the first to use precise cup and spoon measurements in cooking and her teachings were mechanical and practical – not for her any recognition of the enjoyment of the art of cooking. She has been referred to as 'the maiden aunt of home economics'.

When her cookbook first appeared, she had to pay for her own printing and distribution costs as the publishers were so unenthusiastic. Since then it has gone through eleven editions and is still in print.

> *Strange to see how a good dinner and feasting reconciles everybody.*
> Samuel Pepys

Fast Foods   An American senator, Mr S.I. Hayakawa, once lamented the fact that even in Japan – his ancestral home – a fast-food chain had established a hundred eating places. He remarked that it was 'a terrible price to pay for Pearl Harbour'.

England has chicken outlets and hamburger bars imported from the US and a 'restaurant' chain that caters for ten-year-olds who like playing on plastic animals after eating plastic food. There are places that advertise the size of their chef, and fast-food fish and chip joints with a product that tastes as if it had never been near the sea.

Fasting may be better than fast food.

Fennel   There are two forms of fennel – the leafy herb and the root, or bulb.

The herb is a natural with fish. Try a sauce of pernod, cream and fennel for poached white fish – the slightly aniseed flavour of pernod and fennel will probably come as a pleasant surprise.

The bulb is a delicious vegetable which can be braised like celery or quartered, browned lightly in butter and oil and then simmered gently in stock with lemon juice, salt and pepper and a little sugar. It should still have a slight crunch when cooked and is a pleasant change – especially in the winter.

F Fish

Fish

According to the Sea Fish Authority the British eat, as a nation, two pounds (weight) of fish *per household* per year. If the queues at the fish and chip vans at a certain time on a certain day each week are any guide, either some of us are not pulling our weight, or the stuff they sell in soggy batter is not fish.

We live on an island surrounded by a tremendous variety of fresh fish. Yet we eat an awful lot of finger-shaped wedges covered in yellow sawdust trawled from the local supermarket's freezer.

But all this is changing. The tendency now is to be much more aware of the amount of fat in one's diet and of the number of calories eaten. Fish is a dieter's dream, and it is no longer a choice of cod, plaice or haddock only. Hake, monkfish and brill are widely available along with many other varieties which until recently were considered foreign. Even that king of fish, the salmon, is now farmed and much less of a luxury than it used to be.

The following recipe for fish baked in ashes was set down by Archestratus in his *Gastrology* in the 4th century BC:

> **No cheese, no nonsense! Just place it tenderly in fig leaves and tie them on top with a string; then push it under hot ashes bethinking thee wisely of the time when it is done, and burn it not up.**

Keep French dressing in a screw-top jar so it is easy to mix by shaking.

Fondue   If you can't stand the heat, stay out of the fondue. The Swiss are credited with this invention – apparently devised when villages were snowed in and people had to rely on locally-made cheese, wine and bread. It was devised not only as sustenance, but as entertainment as well.

Foodies   The Foodie is a fairly new breed and could be classed as a 'restaurant yuppy'. It spends its free time sampling the delights of every new restaurant which opens, and is probably responsible for closing a few of them. Its conversation is mainly about restaurant menus, and it compares dishes and decor ruthlessly.

Actually the food is not all that important, except as a topic of conversation. The thing is to be seen wherever one should be seen to be eating. Old foodies never die, and they certainly don't fade away!

Fruit Salad   This must surely be the original pudding and is certainly one which has stood the test of time.

It should not be the excuse to use up all the tired over-ripe fruit in the fruit bowl, nor should it come out of a tin, but if it is called 'fruit cocktail' on a menu it almost certainly will.

A real fruit salad is a selection of beautifully prepared, evenly-sliced fruits, including some of the exotic varieties found in most supermarkets now. Give a little thought to colour – nothing but apple, orange and banana will look pale and uninteresting – and resist the temptation to over-sweeten. A dash of liqueur gives a definite lift for a party.

For a change, arrange the sliced fruit in sections on a shallow dish and let people make their own selection. Serve cream and sugar separately, or little pots of melted chocolate to dip into.

G Game

Game

Refers to anything hunted for both sport and food and is an emotive subject in these days of anti-bloodsport campaigns.

Feelings also run high on the serving of game – some people hang it for a very short time and eat it before the 'gamey' flavour has developed very strongly. Others leave it until it drops from a hook of its own accord, when it will probably also walk itself to the oven!

The entrails or 'trail' of birds such as snipe and woodcock are considered a great delicacy. The birds were supposed to be 'passed through a hot oven' and the entrails scraped onto a piece of toast to eat.

One of the most famous misquotations in cookery, 'First catch your hare' came from Mrs Hannah Glass's recipe for jugged hare published in *The Art of Cookery made Plain and Easy* (in 1747). Her actual instructions were to 'take your hare when it is cased' (skinned), but no doubt some people would prefer the misquotation!

Garlic

There's no such thing as a little garlic.
Arthur Baer

Of all good additives, garlic is probably the one that arouses most passion. It is either loved or loathed, and very rarely gives rise to any emotion between those extremes. It has been used in Asian, African and European cuisine for centuries, and often crops up in classical writing.

Aristophanes recorded that athletes used to eat garlic before their exercises at the stadium and Virgil believed that garlic maintained the strength of harvest reapers.

Hippocrates noted that garlic was a laxative and a diuretic but was bad for the eyes, and the prophet Mohammed advised that it should be applied to the bites and stings of poisonous animals.

Pliny believed that it cured consumption, and in the 16th century certain doctors constantly carried several cloves of garlic in their pockets to protect themselves and their patients from bad air and epidemic diseases.

Today garlic is reputed to help in the treatment of rheumatism, fevers, asthma, lip cancer, colds, high blood pressure, skin complaints and many other diseases. If eaten regularly, it's said to keep the body in such a fit state that serious illness is less likely.

Also, as everyone knows, it wards off vampires.

If everything claimed for it is true, it should cure baldness, impotency and just about anything else.

As Ogden Nash put it, 'An apple a day keeps the doctor away; garlic being stronger keeps him away longer.'

Bouquet Garni ● Fresh: 1 bayleaf; 2 sprigs parsley; 1 sprig thyme – tied together.
● Dried: 1 bayleaf; 2 pinches mixed herbs (thyme, marjoram, parsley); 2 cloves; 5 peppercorns – tied in a small piece of muslin.

George IV   Of all royalty, probably George IV had the worst reputation for gluttony. By 1820, when he came to the throne, he was grossly obese.

It was reported that his coronation finished with a banquet for 312 peers of the realm who were served soup, fish, hot joints, vegetables, shellfish, braised ham, goose, savoury pies, cakes, braised beef and capons, cold lamb and fowl.

There were almost 1,200 side dishes to this repast, and some 700 dishes of pastry, jellies and creams. The peeresses would lower baskets from the gallery above, hoping that their husbands would share a little with them.

G German Cuisine

George IV – A voluptuary under the horrors of digestion

Extravagances, gluttony and callousness made George IV a weak-minded king, and during the closing years of his life he kept almost entirely to his overheated apartment where he drank vast quantities of cherry brandy. He suffered from delusions brought about by his excesses and believed he actually commanded a battalion at Waterloo.

While he was still Prince Regent, the future George IV quarrelled violently with that celebrated leader of fashion, Beau Brummel. Some time after that quarrel the Prince encountered Brummel and a friend while out riding. Brummel was pointedly ignored by HRH. As the Prince rode away, Brummel demanded of his companion, in a voice loud enough to be heard by the departing Regent, 'Who's your fat friend?' Brummel was thereafter ostracised from English Society.

German Cuisine

German food is not the 'wurst' in Europe, but it is probably the heaviest. Their breads – like rye and pumpernickel – are dark and rich; sauerkraut (not a rude German but pickled cabbage fermented in brine) is served with practically everything. Dumplings also appear with great regularity.

The sausages are wonderful and the venison is particularly good. Sauerbraten is the best known beef casserole, and smoked fish such as the Baltic herring is a particular favourite. German cakes, fancy breads and biscuits are plentiful, and irresistible.

The wines have a distinctive sweetness, and the great dessert wines – Auslese, Trockenbeerenauslese and Eiswein – are unique. It is mostly the very ordinary wines that are imported into Britain.

Mark Twain, for one, was unimpressed: 'The Germans are exceedingly fond of Rhine wines; they are put up in tall slender bottles and are considered a pleasant beverage. One tells them from vinegar by the label.'

> *Cuisine is when things taste like themselves.*
> *Curnonsky*

German Wines

If for no other reason than the pleasure of reciting the names, a knowledge of German wines is a good thing.

In order of excellence they go:

Tafelwein	– table wine, normally blended
Qualitatswein	– from a single defined area
Qualitatswein mit Pradikat	– of known and proven quality
Kabinett	– generally higher-quality wines
Spatelese	– from grapes picked after the main harvest
Auslese	– from fully ripened and mature grapes only
Beerenauslese	– from selected overripe fruit – often with 'noble rot'
Trockenbeerenauslese	– selected shrivelled fruit of the highest taste concentration. Very rare
Eiswein	– grapes frozen to ice, picked and pressed whilst frozen

Try saying all that on a packet of wine gums!

When making brown or granary bread, crack an egg into the mixture. It will give a moister loaf.

G Gin

> *Serenely full the epicure may say,*
> *Fate cannot harm me.*
> *I have dined today.*
> Sydney Smith

Gin

In the middle of the 17th century a Dutchman, Francescus de la Boe, distilled spirits with the juice of juniper berries and thereby invented a new alcoholic drink.

English seamen and traders discovered its delights and brought it into England. A few souls started to distill it at home and it was then given the name gin, from the Dutch word *geneva* meaning 'juniper berry'.

It was more of a potion than a drink to be enjoyed. Those who could afford it drank French brandy and the ordinary people stuck to beer and cider.

In 1688 William and Mary gained the throne and, in an attempt both to stop people drinking brandy imported from an unfriendly power and to encourage farmers to grow more cereal crops, the populace was given the freedom to distill alcohol from English grain.

The results were disastrous. It was reported that one house in five in the City of London sold gin. In 1727 the annual consumption was three million gallons. Fifteen years later it was nineteen million gallons! The population of London at that time was about 100,000, meaning that on average six pints of mother's ruin was drunk per head per week. Signs advertised oblivion thus: 'Drunk for a penny, dead drunk for twopence; clean straw for nothing.'

Ginger

Either you love ginger or you hate it, but no-one is indifferent about it. In the Middle Ages a pound of ginger had the same value as a sheep (probably because it was supposed to be an aphrodisiac) but happily it is not so expensive now. Nonetheless, crystallised and preserved ginger is still quite a luxury. Much of the processing of the ginger root has to be done by hand because of its uneven shape, and the cooking process takes place over several days, during which time increasingly-large doses of sugar syrup are fed to the ginger and slowly absorbed.

Most supermarkets now sell fresh ginger, which has a wonderful fragrance and will make a quick and exotic sauce for fish or chicken. Just melt some butter, add lemon or lime juice and simmer until syrupy – add a dash of cream and plenty of grated ginger, and just pray that your guests love it too!

> *Music with dinner is an insult to both the cook and the violinist.*
> *G.K. Chesterton*

Gourmet or Gourmand

The gourmet is a connoisseur of food and wines, while the gourmand's chief pleasure is eating for its own sake.

The gourmet thus respects quality; the gourmand quantity.

Originally the gourmet was a sworn official charged with the duty of tasting wines and spirits. A gastronome (not one of these gadgets which sit on top of a piano during music lessons) is a pedantic term for an expert in gastronomy.

Grog

It was only in 1971 that the Royal Navy did away with the practice of issuing a diluted rum ration to the sailors.

Admiral Vernon was called 'Old Grog' by his sailors as he always wore a grogram (taffeta) cloak in rough weather. He was the first to serve water in the rum on board ship, and the mixture went by the name of grog.

H **Haggis**

Haggis   Devised on Scottish farms to use up the lungs, heart and liver of a
                  sheep, haggis is nothing more than a mutton sausage. The stomach
                  forms the casing and minced heart, liver and lights – together with
                  suet, onions and oatmeal – form the stuffing.

                  This dish may be regarded as the national dish of Scotland and is
                  traditionally served on Burns' Night, when it's piped to the table
                  accompanied by Roberts Burns' *Address to a Haggis*.

> *Fair fa' you honest sonsie face,*
> *Great chieftain o' the puddin' race.*

                  It should be served with *clapshot,* that is *tatties and neeps* (otherwise
                  known as potatoes with turnips) and accompanied by neat single malt
                  whisky.

                  According to Hugh MacDiarmid:

> *You canna gang to a Burns supper*
> *even*
> *Wi'oot some wizened scrunt o' a*
> *knock knee*
> *Chinee turns roon to say, 'Him*
> *Haggis – velly goot'.*
> *And ten to wan the piper is a*
> *cockney.*

Dog

Hair of the   The ancient Romans believed that 'like cures like', and therefore
Dog   thought that a drink would cure the effects of the last bout of drink-
                  ing. The expression was originally 'a hair of the dog that bit you' and
                  referred to an imaginary cure for people bitten by a rabid dog. To avoid
                  hydrophobia they ate the burnt hair of the dog that had bitten them
                  – if they could catch it.

                  There is no real evidence that more drink will cure a hangover, but
                  there is no doubt that it can help sometimes. In his diary, Samuel Pepys
                  says he himself tried it and found it effective. In the entry for August
                  3, 1661, he records an aching head as a result of the previous night's
                  carousing. His friends made him drink from the same wine that caused
                  his condition, telling him it would help – 'Which I thought strange,
                  but I think find true.'

There are ready-made proprietary cures available and some people swear by Bloody Marys and the Bullshot. But it's the Prairie Oyster which has perhaps the greatest following.

Break an egg into a glass, keeping the egg intact. Add a teaspoon each of wine vinegar and Worcester sauce, some salt and cayenne pepper and toss it down in one swallow.

It doubles as breakfast too.

If you cannot face that in the morning, drink lots of liquid before you go to bed and a bottle of cola of some sort to quell the queasy stomach the next day.

Only aspirin and time will get rid of the headache.

Ham

A great British tradition! When hams were home cured, or bought from a local butcher, the meat was firm, moist and pink with a wonderful smoky aroma and many subtle flavours which varied from county to county, as each had its favourite recipe for curing. The wet, flabby and uniformly-shaped slices on sale today might have come from a completely different animal.

The curing recipes varied, but all required one vital ingredient – time. Having chosen a leg from 'a hog that is fat and well fed', it was then hung, sprinkled with various salts for several days, then turned for anything up to five weeks. Sometimes black treacle or stale beer was used too.

The dried hams had bran or chaff thrown over them and were consigned to the chimney to be smoked. If properly cured they could last for up to a year, but the housewife was advised in warm weather to 'pepper some pillow cases', put the ham inside, and hang them where 'there is a nice air blowing'.

Use a pastry brush to remove grated lemon or orange peel from the grater.

Herbs and Spices

Herbs are the dried leaves of aromatic plants. Their flavour disappears with age.

Spices are usually the seeds, bark or seed cover of a plant, and are often bought ground.

H Hodge's Grace

Hodge's Grace   'Hodge' was a familiar and condescending term for a farm labourer or peasant. The famous Hodge's Grace could be used before a *Cuisine Minceur* meal:

> *Heavenly Father bless us, and keep us all alive,*
> *There's ten of us for dinner, and not enough for five.*

Home-made Wine   One should never be ashamed of making home-made wine. It is a thing that should be tried – once. After that leave it to the experts. They know what they are doing and how to do it.

To give it to guests can be embarrassing, particularly if they're asked to give their honest opinion of the latest parsnip and pumpkin seed concoction. Most guests are well-bred enough to utter some vague generalities while trying surreptitiously to pour the glass into the nearest pot plant. However, one day someone will tell the truth and that will be the end of a beautiful friendship.

Home on the Range   In 1780 Thomas Robinson patented a kitchen range. It had a cast iron oven lined with bricks, and contained shelves on one side and a boiler for heating water on the other.

Then, in 1802, George Bodley of Exeter patented a cooking range with a closed top that became the prototype for all later models. The built-in ones were called 'kitchen ranges'; those free-standing with a flue were called 'kitcheners'.

The first gas cooker appeared in 1824, and in 1841 the chef at London's Reform Club installed the first gas ranges in a restaurant kitchen.

Electric ranges were introduced in the 1890s and were very popular because, unlike the gas ranges and solid fuel cookers, they cooked cleanly.

Today's kitchen ranges are large affairs of thin metal with four separate hobs (some of which even work), two ovens (neither of which ever reach the correct heat), plastic controls which tell the cooking temperature to the nearest 100 degrees and a clock that is right at least twice a day.

Honey

> *I eat my peas with honey,*
> *I've done it all my life;*
> *It makes them taste quite funny*
> *But it keeps them on my knife*
> *Anon*

Until the middle of the 18th century when the West Indian sugar trade flourished, honey was the main sweetening agent. A jar found in an Egyptian tomb was still recognisable after 5000 years, and the Greeks believed it was associated with fertility.

The word 'honeymoon' originated from a Teutonic custom whereby a newly-married couple would live on honey from their wedding day until the first full moon, in order to ensure a large and happy family.

Pooh Bear loved honey, of course, and wrote a 'pome' about it in A. A. Milne's *Winnie the Pooh:*

> *Isn't it funny*
> *How a bear likes honey,*
> *Buzz, buzz, buzz,*
> *I wonder why he does?*

As well as being delicious to eat, honey is said to have medicinal properties external as well as internal, for germs cannot live in it.

It is also used in beauty preparations and taken as an instant source of energy.

It has been calculated that 550 bees have to visit two-and-a-half million flowers to produce one pound of honey, but with all its many properties perhaps their efforts are worthwhile.

Hors d'oeuvre

By definition these snacks are additional to the menu. The name does not actually come from the kitchen but from architecture.

Early architectural blueprints showed only the main structure. Any outbuildings were omitted and were technically designated 'outside the work' – in French, *hors d'oeuvre.*

When chefs wished to offer an appetiser to be served before the meal they chose this same term because these preliminary offerings were outside their own main work – the meal itself.

Hot Cross Buns

| Hot Cross Buns | It is said that these buns were made of the dough kneaded for the 'Host', the consecrated bread of the church representing the Body of Christ. These were, accordingly, marked with the cross. |

Hot Cross Buns   It is said that these buns were made of the dough kneaded for the 'Host', the consecrated bread of the church representing the Body of Christ. These were, accordingly, marked with the cross.

However, their origins may date back further. According to ancient Greek beliefs, the round bun represents the full moon and the cross symbolises the four quarters. They were made in honour of the goddess Diana.

These Good Friday buns are supposed to keep for 12 months without turning mouldy, although it might be unwise to test this.

> *I've made it a rule never to drink by daylight and never to refuse a drink after dark.*
> H.L. Mencken

Humble Pie   'To eat humble pie' has come to mean that you should swallow your pride and beg for forgiveness.

Umbles was once a common description of offal. These bits of a carcass used to be credited with little culinary worth, fit only to be made into pies for servants and the poor.

In time 'umbles' became an obsolete word, its meaning forgotten, but it lived on in 'to eat humble pie'. The 'h' was added in ignorance of the pie's true origin, and in the reasonable assumption that the correct word was 'humble'.

Hunt Ball   Often a case of the unspeakable eating the inedible!

The Hunt Ball is a favourite haunt of bun-flinging Hooray Henrys who turn the meal into a battlefield for the guest and an obstacle course for the waitresses.

Prawn heads and menu cards make wonderful missiles, as do balls of soggy bread and plates of creamy pudding. But confronted with the offerings of mass catering, who can blame them?

Roll chopped glacé cherries in flour before adding them to cake mixtures to prevent them sinking.

Ice

Ice

Is it because of the cold British climate that it's often impossible to get, even on the hottest day of the summer, ice in a drink in the local pub? Huge inns have one small ice bucket to serve four bars. Ask for lots of ice, and the response is usually a couple of half-melted cubes if you're lucky.

For the many thousands who have no idea how to make ice, here is an infallible recipe: to one refrigerator freezer compartment add one ice cube tray filled with water. (Water is available in most homes.) Freeze and use when needed.

> **When men reach their 60s and retire they go to pieces. Women just go right on cooking.**
> **Gail Sheehy**

Insects – Edible

A few years ago there was a craze for eating sugar-coated ants and chocolate covered bees – or it may have been the other way round. In some countries, however, insects are very much a part of the normal diet. As they feed mainly on the green stuff which is the diet of man and his flocks and herds, it isn't really surprising.

In Arab countries, Africa and Asia, insects are a delicacy, although these people would shudder at the thought of eating shellfish!

White ants are particularly good and, not so long ago, fried grasshoppers and cicadas were still appreciated in sunny climes. Cicada essence is a wonderful addition to soups and stews and the Chinese love the chrysalis of the silkworm. In Mexico fried palm and agave grubs are sold from the street barrows like roast chestnuts.

> **Plain cooking cannot be entrusted to plain cooks.**
> **Countess Morphy**

International Cuisine

The sign to avoid if you really want to sample the local dishes when on holiday.

It either means you will be served an anglicised version of moussaka, paella or lasagne (usually with chips and peas) or the Greek, Spanish or Italian version of roast beef and Yorkshire pudding.

One thing is for sure: it will certainly not be the best of *any* country's cuisine.

Kebab K

Irish Coffee   A great deal of whiskey, coffee, time and temper can be wasted trying to produce the perfect Irish coffee.

Give up pouring the cream over the back of a spoon and ending up with white coffee. Float whipped cream on top instead and make the end result alcoholic enough to ensure that nobody complains.

> *Never commit yourself to a cheese without having first examined it.*
> **T.S. Eliot**

Jelly   Whether the subject is the pudding or the boiled, clear jam variety there is always the same problem – will it set?

If the first one doesn't, pour it over sponge cakes, add some fruit, alcohol, custard and cream and call it a trifle anyway.

If the second doesn't, it can be boiled all over again, spoonfuls added to sauces and gravies, or warmed and poured over ice-cream. So whatever the outcome, it isn't a major disaster!

Junket   Junket is the perfect invalid food and can either be eaten or applied to the afflicted part!

The name for this curdled cream mix comes from the Latin for 'rush', *juncus*, as it was originally made in rush baskets.

A junket is also a dainty sweetmeat, cake or confection, often served at feasts. By abbreviation it came to mean the feast itself and, in the United States, any outing at which eating and drinking took place.

Use a potato peeler on chocolate at room temperature to make long chocolate curls for decorating cakes and puddings.

Juniper   The main flavouring ingredient for gin, the juniper berry is supposed to have strong medicinal properties. 'Genever' or Dutch gin was first made as a medicine to treat heart, kidney and bladder disorders. In country areas a few drops of juniper oil on a sugar cube are still used as a cure for backache.

This is also the flavouring to use with game, particularly pheasant.

Kebab   Nearly every High Street in Britain can now boast its kebab house – though the dry tasteless meat and cardboard-like pitta bread which they offer are usually a far cry from the real thing.

K **Kellogg, Dr John Harvey**

Kebabs should be made from succulent chunks of meat, fish, fruit or vegetables threaded on skewers and cooked over a barbecue or under a grill.

The idea is thought to have originated in the Caucasus where the mountain people speared pieces of meat on their swords and held them over open fires to cook.

The dish spread to Turkey, Greece, Middle Eastern countries, India and Asia, and now has many variations. If the meat is marinaded, to add extra flavour and to tenderise it, it can be a delicious addition to a summer barbecue.

Kellogg, Dr John Harvey

> *The breakfast food idea made its appearance in a little third storey room in New York City. My cooking facilities were very limited ... It often occurred to me that it should be possible to purchase cereals at groceries already cooked and ready to eat, and I considered different ways in which this might be done.*

So wrote J. H. Kellogg, a physician, health food pioneer and vegetarian. In 1876 he became superintendent of the Seventh Day Adventist Western Health Reform Sanitarium and developed numerous nut and vegetable products to vary the diet of his patients – including the now-famous and very-much-copied corn flakes. His brother, Will, formed the W. K. Kellogg Company to manufacture those breakfast foods.

Kettle of Fish Early picnics often featured salmon as the main dish. The party would choose a spot by the river where salmon were most likely to be hooked. A large cauldron would be placed on a fire, salt added to the water – and the caught salmon dropped in and boiled.

When the fish was cooked, the party would eat it gypsy fashion – handed round and eaten with the fingers.

The discomfort of eating in this way probably gave rise to the phrase 'a pretty kettle of fish'.

Always whip egg whites at room temperature and not when just out of the fridge.

Kickshaws   A lovely word, not in general use today, meaning made dishes, odds and ends, dainty trifles of little value.

Originally written 'kickshose' a corruption of the French *quelque chose* (something), the kickshaw was immortalised by Shakespeare in *Henry IV Part II:*

> *Some pigeons Davy, a couple of short-legged hens, a joint of mutton and any pretty little tiny kickshaws.*

Kir   If you are unfortunate enough to buy a bottle of white wine which seems thin, acidic and decidedly uninteresting, add a little *crème de cassis* (a low-alcohol blackcurrant cordial) or, failing that, blackcurrant syrup. The result – a glass that is at worst drinkable and at best delicious.

Traditionally, Bourgogne Aligote – a white Burgundy of lesser distinction than Chablis – is used for Kir, but it should be made only with very dry wine.

Kir Cardinale, on the other hand, is made with red wine, while Kir Royale is a more up-market version, made using non-vintage champagne instead of white wine.

Kiwi Fruit   Not, as the name implies, originally from New Zealand, but imported there in the 19th century from China. More properly known as Chinese gooseberries, they have been adopted with glee by the *nouvelle cuisine* movement.

They are lovely for decoration, provided they are skinned, but they taste a bit like rubber. Probably the most over-rated fruit on the market.

Ladies First   The English custom of the ladies leaving the men at the table at the end of the meal was considered barbaric elsewhere in Europe. Possibly it stemmed from the time when the preparation of tea and coffee was a matter of ceremony, and the ladies would withdraw in advance to prepare the beverage.

L Lamb

Men drank very heavily then, and would continue to sit around the table for hours consuming many bottles of port. They were generally in no condition to join the ladies anyway.

Lamb Sir Walter Scott, prolific author of tales of chivalry and old Scotland, was a true romantic.

One spring morning he was walking around his Abbotsford estate accompanied by Lady Scott when they passed a field of frolicking lambs.

'No wonder that poets from the earliest times have made lambs the symbols of peace and innocence,' remarked Scott.

'Delightful creatures indeed,' agreed his wife. 'Especially with mint sauce.'

> *I do not think that anything serious should be done after dinner, as nothing should be before breakfast .*
> **George Saintsbury**

Larder A very peculiar word is larder, with rather bloodthirsty overtones. It actually comes from the old French *lardoir,* which meant a storeplace for bacon.

In 1307 the companion in arms to Robert Bruce, Lord James Douglas, recaptured his castle and garrison from its English occupiers. He then gathered together all the English captives and their supplies, scattered all the food and beer over the floor in a great heap, slaughtered the prisoners and cast their bodies on to the pile. This he called 'the Douglas Larder' in derision of the English.

Lemon Sole The name of this flat fish has nothing to do with lemon at all, but comes from the French *limande* which means a flat board.

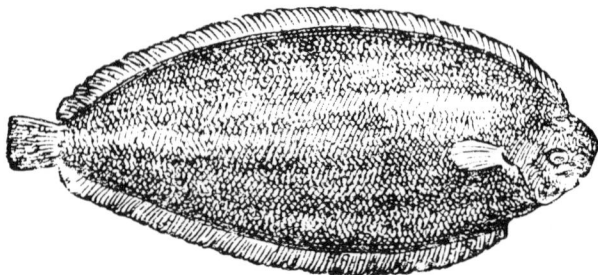

| Lips That Touch Wine . . . | According to Robert Benchley, 'Drinking makes such fools of people and people are such fools to begin with that it is compounding a felony.' |

According to Robert Benchley, 'Drinking makes such fools of people and people are such fools to begin with that it is compounding a felony.'

A touch severe, but justified at times. The story stumbled through drunkenly with the punchline totally forgotten – or the awful awakening the morning after with dry mouth, a throbbing head and a feeling that a phone call to apologise is called for – perhaps bear out Benchley's comment. Such lapses, though unfortunate, teach nothing and the odd glass that refreshes is still welcome.

Over the centuries, the subject of drink has inspired many a witticism. W.C. Fields, for example, once grunted; 'I never drink water – fish fornicate in it', a bit extreme perhaps, while Oscar Wilde more reasonably commented, 'Now and again it is a joy to have one's table red with wine and roses'. Almost a century earlier Samuel Johnson had observed, 'The feeling of friendship is like that of being comfortably filled with roast beef; love, like being enlivened with champagne'.

And there are other uses for the wine, too:

Lady at dinner party:
You mean to tell me that you never ever let water touch your lips? Then what do you use to clean your teeth, pray?
Gentleman:
A light Sauterne, madame.

The moral is, perhaps: 'Eat, drink and be merry – for tomorrow we diet'. (And as we know so well, tomorrow is the day after yesterday, and it never comes . . .)

Liqueurs

To many, a perfect end to a good meal, liqueurs are merely spirits which have been flavoured with fruits, herbs, roots and plants and sweetened with sugar syrup. Sometimes they are artificially coloured. The best originate from monasteries. Monks collected the herbs, then alchemists and medical specialists of the monastery developed liqueurs, primarily as medicines.

Liqueur is an abbreviation of the old French *liqueur de dessert,* which simply means 'sweet liquid'. The best of them are made by steeping the flavouring materials in a spirit. When the spirit is well impregnated with these flavours it is distilled in a pot still. The number of flavourings varies from liqueur to liqueur. Chartreuse, for example, has at least 130 herbs – more than any other liqueur.

L Lobster

One should never eat when drinking a liqueur – after all, they are digestives. Restaurants sell them in little glasses full to the brim, which is a shame because the bouquet is part of the pleasure. Ask the waiter next time to put the same quantity in a small balloon glass, and perhaps appreciate the whole drink as one would brandy or whisky.

Don't forget, however, that they're very potent and should be treated with respect.

Lobster

An extremely delicious and very expensive crustacean, lobster is often ruined by being smothered with a cheese sauce. This shellfish needs to be treated delicately and with a great deal of respect.

Served cold with a little mayonnaise and salad it's a wonderful summer lunch dish. Served hot as devilled lobster, it's superb.

For each person:

Sauté a little onion and celery in a good amount of butter. Add this to a good handful of breadcrumbs. Mix a teaspoonful of dry English mustard, cayenne pepper, as much Worcester sauce as you can stand, milk to moisten and enough chopped parsley to add colour. Stir in the coarsely chopped, cooked flesh of a medium sized lobster, pile back into the shell, dot with more butter, cook in a moderate oven until the top is browning (20 – 30 minutes) and serve – preferably with a Chablis or Pouilly Fumé.

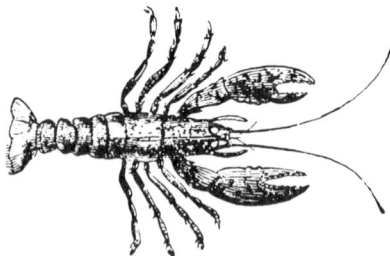

In some restaurants you can still find live lobsters on display in a tank. The 19th-century French playwright, Georges Feydeau, was once served a lobster with only one claw. Asking why, he was told that the creatures often fight in the tank – and this one had lost a claw in a tussle.

'Take this one away,' said Feydeau, 'and bring me the victor.'

Actually despatching a lobster is a task reserved for the brave. It's done either by sticking a knife into the base of its head, thus severing the nerves; or placing it in a pan of water and bringing it to the boil. The lobster will fall asleep first. Lobsters should never, never be dropped into boiling water.

Magna Carta It was written into the Magna Carta in 1215 that there was to be a standard measure for wine and ale. Before that many ale-houses had communal drinking vessels which were passed around, and there was little regulation as to amounts served.

In 750 the Archbishop of York issued an edict banning his priests from frequenting ale-houses, and some 200 years later King Edgar restricted public houses to one per village.

By 1276 a gallon of ale cost three farthings or, if it was a particularly good brew, one penny.

A rubber band around the lid of a tightly-closed jar makes it easy to turn and open.

Mange Tout To paraphrase Shirley Conran, life is too short to stuff a mange tout. But if you must: blanch it, open carefully, pipe in a cream cheese and garlic mixture, sprinkle with paprika and stand back for applause.

Mango This delicious fruit is readily available in supermarkets and green-grocers, and is ripe when very soft and fragrant. The flesh makes a delicious sauce for ice-cream if you purée it with lemon juice and a little sugar; cut into cubes it mixes well with cold chicken and mayonnaise for a summer salad.

Best of all is a really ripe mango, eaten just as it is, preferably in the bath as it will be very messy. Eaten in the raw, so to speak . . .

And most, dear actors, eat no onions nor garlic for we are to utter sweet breath.
Shakespeare

Marinade The idea of a marinade is to give extra flavour to food – and, in the case of meat, to tenderise it and prevent it from drying during the cooking process. The word comes from the French *marinar* (to pickle in brine) and it is quite possible to leave food in a marinade for a few days if it is kept cool. It will improve considerably the texture and flavour of cheaper cuts of meat.

Seasoning, spices, herbs, oil and wine or lemon juice are the main ingredients of a marinade, and they can usually be added to the dish in place of other liquids. If you're barbecuing, the marinade can be brushed over the food while it's cooking.

M Marjoram

The problem with a marinade is that it demands foresight on the part of the chef. Such forward planning is all too rare – the recipe chosen tends to be a last minute choice and even then only cursorily read by the confident chef. It is only on taking the first bite, and noticing guests wince, that the mistake becomes apparent. To turn leather into succulent meat, the dish should, of course, have been marinating for 24 hours . . .

Marjoram

A very pungent and aromatic herb good in casseroles, braised meat dishes and sausages as well as with fish and vegetables. It is widely used in Italian cookery, especially in pizzas.

It's been known as a culinary herb since Roman times, and was later valued highly by the Elizabethans as a strewing herb, in pot pourri, and as a cure for almost everything from insomnia to sea sickness.

Prepare double quantities of meat for coarse pâtés, steak and kidney pies and casseroles – and freeze it uncooked. It tastes much better than a reheated cooked dish

Marmalade

Marmalade, so it is said, goes back to classical times and to an unknown Greek who grafted cuttings from an apple tree onto a quince. He produced a fruit which he called honey apple – *melimelon* in his Greek tongue. Although today marmalade is made primarily from oranges, its name still echoes the honey apple from which it was originally made.

But there's also a different story of how this confection received its name. Tradition has it that when Mary Queen of Scots fell ill and refused all food, her worried household recalled a certain jam – then a rare delicacy – which Her Majesty relished. With this they tempted her appetite – and Mary ate. Such was their relief that her retinue named the jam 'sick Mary' or, in the fashionable court French of the time, *Marie malade.*

Yet another contender for the source of the word is the Portuguese *marmelo,* meaning 'quince'.

The tale is told too of a Dundee merchant in the early 18th century who bought a cargo of Seville oranges from a Spanish ship forced by storms to seek shelter in Dundee harbour. The oranges were too bitter and no-one wanted to buy them. His wife, however – not wanting to waste the fruit – boiled them for jam. And thus the famous Dundee orange marmalade was born.

Masquerade at Ranelagh

On Tuesday night last a Masqued Ball was given at this place which, to excite curiosity at the expense of candour, was announced to be an imitation of a Venetian Carnival. Except in the execrable quality and, as the Irishman said, the plentiful scarcity of the wines, and the usual dullness of the company, we really could not observe any difference between this foreign imitation and a common English masquerade, at the usual and sufficient price of ONE GUINEA.
About one o'clock a few feeble voices, accompanied by a feeble band, sang an Ode in honour of the Duke of York's marriage; but this tribute of loyalty was so little attended to that it might have as well been ... any other composition.
At two o'clock, the buffets were opened, and the company regaled with a cold collation which, except for a few ices, was marked with no peculiar distinction; and the Burgundy, which was the only wine in any degree fit to make use of, being almost immediately exhausted, the supper-eaters were happy in an opportunity of diluting with a tankard or two of Whitbread's brown butt.
The Observer
February 19, 1792

Mayonnaise

When the Duc de Richelieu captured Port Mahon, Minorca, in 1756 he demanded food. There being little but eggs and oil he beat them up together – hence the original *mahon-naise*.

The recipe sounds easy. Beat pepper, salt, oil, vinegar, yolk of an egg together, and mayonnaise should result. Far easier said than done, but if you have a blender it is well worth trying because if it curdles it can easily be rescued. Just pour out the curdled mixture, add another egg to the blender and start the whole process again, pouring the mixture in very slowly.

In the summer add parsley, watercress and some chives to make a cool, green mayonnaise – very pretty with buffet food – or try using an avocado and just one egg yolk to make a spectacular avocado mayonnaise. Delicious with hard boiled eggs.

M Menuspeak

Menuspeak   Restaurant menus can be intimidating affairs, often in flowery French for the purpose of confusing the customer with a plethora of unfamiliar or half-remembered expressions. The following are among the more common:

Anglaise – garnish of boiled vegetables.

Au gratin – cooked with breadcrumbs or cheese on top, then browned under the grill.

Béchamel – white sauce of butter and flour mixed with milk, and sometimes with herbs and diced vegetables.

Blanquette – dish cooked with white sauce.

Bouchée – small vol-au-vent.

Bouillon – broth.

Bourguignon – sauce with red burgundy, button mushrooms and baby onions.

Brochettes – pieces of meat on a skewer.

Chasseur – sautéed mushrooms added to sauté of chicken, veal etc.

Clarify – to cleanse impurities in butter by heating, or in broth by using the white of an egg.

Colbert – sauce containing meat or fish glaze, stock, butter, lemon juice, Madeira and parsley.

Compote – fruit poached in sugar syrup.

Concasser – skinned, seeded tomatoes cut into thin strips.

Demi-glâce – brown sauce made from diced vegetables, tomato purée, mushrooms and bouquet garni.

Duxelles – finely chopped mushrooms and shallots.

Florentine – garnish of spinach.

Fricassée – pieces of cooked white meat reheated in a creamy white sauce.

Hollandaise – hot sauce containing egg yolks, butter and lemon juice.

Jardiniere – groups of different vegetables used to garnish meat dishes – usually with demi-glace sauce.

Lardons – finger-sized strips of bacon used for flavouring.

Lyonnaise – garnish of fried onions.

Macedoine – mixture of vegetables or fruit cut into large dice.

Meunière – finish of butter and lemon juice.

Milanese – pasta with tomato sauce, shredded ham and mushrooms.

Mirepoix – selection of diced vegetables in equal quantities.

Mornay – béchamel sauce flavoured with cheese.

Noisette – best end of neck of lamb boned, seasoned, tied into a roll and cut into one-and-a-half inch thick slices.

Normande – garnish of cider, apples, butter and cream; or, with sole, garnish of mussels, oysters, shrimps and mushrooms.

Roux – mixture of flour and fat used as a base for sauce or soup.

St Germain – garnish of peas.

Suprême – breast of chicken.

Meringues   A meringue is simplicity itself – pure egg white and sugar whipped together. So many people, though, find them impossible to make. Here are a few tips.

Don't use very fresh eggs. Put the whites, at room temperature, into a scrupulously clean glass or metal bowl (they will not whip stiffly if grease is present). Whip until they look as if they are ready – then carry on for a couple of minutes longer. Whisk in half the quantity of sugar until the mixture is shiny (not too long or it collapses), then fold in the other half.

Spread or pipe the mixture onto silicone paper and cook for a very long time in the lowest possible oven – they can even be left overnight. Finally, store them somewhere warm and dry (the airing cupboard is ideal), otherwise they will go sticky and collapse.

Once you've mastered the knack, a whole range of marvellous puds opens up.

For a crisp skin on baked potatoes, rub with a little oil or butter and sprinkle with salt before baking. A metal skewer pushed through the potato will conduct heat to the centre and help cook it more quickly.

Michelin   André Michelin, along with his brother, was responsible for inventing the first detachable pneumatic cycle tyre.

When the first car to use his tyre was manufactured in 1895, he decided to produce a guide to provide tourists in France with information about places they might visit. Free with the car in 1900 came the first Michelin Guide, with information about where to eat and sleep – and buy petrol and spare parts – in 1,200 alphabetically-named towns. Restaurants considered exceptionally worthy were given the now famous knife-and-fork and star symbols.

As the tyre company grew, the range of Michelin Guides expanded to cover Europe and North Africa. The first guide to cover Britain and Ireland was produced in 1911, covering more than 1,500 towns in the format which is now an institution. It listed their hotels and garages as well as information on motor law, taxation, the whereabouts of hospitals, post offices and railway stations.

Michelin held that there were only two types of cooking – good and bad. For this, his famous three-star rating scale was more than enough! Many have copied him since, but it's thanks to André Michelin that standards were set to ensure that guides would be genuinely critical.

M Milk before Tea

Milk before Tea It is generally known as an old-fashioned habit to put milk in the cup before pouring the tea, but the habit has its basis in practicality.

In the late 17th century, when tea was imported from China it was quite appropriately served in bowls from that country. Thinking that the tea might crack the delicate china they cooled it down by pouring in cold milk first.

Heat-resistant china and more solid cups are now the norm, but the habit persists.

> *Where there's smoke there's toast.*
> **Anon**

Mint There are at least fourteen varieties of mint grown in Britain, the most common being peppermint and spearmint. As well as using it with new potatoes and peas and in mint sauce, try it in meatballs made with lamb, in salads, wine cups and, of course, mint juleps.

The name comes from Mintha, who in Greek mythology was loved by Pluto. When his jealous wife, Persephone, found out she transformed the poor girl into a herb.

It is widely used as a digestive but in Tunisia you will be offered a strong, dark, mint tea with pine kernels that's more likely to give you indigestion than cure it!

> *All I ask of food is that it doesn't harm me.*
> **Michael Palin**

Monosodium Glutamate (MSG) A white crystalline substance, MSG is used primarily in Chinese and Japanese cooking as a food additive and to enhance flavours. It is called Vetsin, Ajinomoto, Taste Powder and even P'sst. It should be used very sparingly as large quantities can be dangerous, triggering an allergic reaction characterised by chest pains and a burning feeling.

A pinch of brown sugar or a stock cube is a safer alternative.

To rescue a casserole or stew which is burning, dip the pan quickly into cold water. This will make the meat leave the bottom of the pan.

Mustard   Mustard originated in the Mediterranean and Middle East, and is even mentioned in the Bible.

The early Egyptians used dried mustard as a condiment and Cleopatra was reputed to sprinkle it in her bath to invigorate her.

The ancient Romans, who used it extensively, imported it into Gaul where it became so popular that there was even a guild of mustard makers in the 15th century.

The Romans also introduced it to Britain where it was made into a thick paste and mixed with vinegar before use.

Traditional English mustard, with its fiery taste, was invented in the 1720s. French mustard is normally either Dijon (mixed with juice from unripened grapes), Bordeaux (mixed with fermented wine), or Meaux (whole grain blended with herbs and spices).

German mustard is normally sweet, mild and herby, and Italian has candied fruits in a mixture of mustard and sugar syrup.

(On a less tasteful note, the oil extracted from black mustard seeds was a prime ingredient of World War I's potentially-lethal mustard gas.)

But you don't have to actually eat lots of mustard to keep its makers happy. George Colman, founder of the Colman empire, is reputed to have said, 'I make my profit not by the mustard people use, but from what they leave on their plates.'

> *Good manners: the noise you don't make when you're eating soup.*
> **Bennett Cerf**

Nettles   Although cursed as a garden weed, nettles do have their uses.

They are gathered by country folk to be used as a spring green or a seasoning, and to make soup or tea. The 'devil's leaf' marked the place where elves lived and in Anglo-Saxon times the nettle was considered to be a sacred herb. The 17th-century diaries of Samuel Pepys mention nettle porridge, and in Queen Anne's time powdered nettle was taken as snuff.

Nettle beer used to be popular. Indeed the great herbalist, Culpepper, claimed that 'it killeth worms in children, easeth pains in the sides, and dissolveth the windiness in the spleen'.

N **Noble Rot**

Noble Rot
(Botrytis
Cinerea)

This is the priceless mould which grows on some grapes and concentrates their sugar content. The grapes are picked late, when they have shrivelled, and from them come some outstanding dessert wines like the French Sauternes and the German Auseleses.

Cheap sweet wine, on the other hand, is assuredly not made from grapes with 'noble rot'. It's merely cheap wine, and usually very nasty. Perhaps if one's taste is for very sweet liquids it would be cheaper to drink lemonade . . .

> **Mustard's no good without roast beef.**
> Chico Marx

Notices

Customers who consider our waitresses uncivil should see our manager. (Notice in a cafe)

This packet of ready-made pastry will make enough for four persons or twelve tarts. (Advice on a food package)

Enjoy our large airy rooms for small families. Home-type food, diets catered for, homemade muffins, country fresh eggs. Hospital is the aim here. (From a travel leaflet)

I always notice when I buy your product the top biscuit is broken. I am therefore writing to suggest that in future you leave out the top biscuit. (From a letter to a biscuit manufacturer)

By and by, God caught his eye. (On a gravestone for a waiter)

The management advises that no refunds will be given to patrons whose meals are eaten by seagulls. (Notice beside a seaside resataurant)

Make your plans for the day while enjoying a healthy full English breakfast served by our friendly and courteous staff. If you are still with us at lunchtime join the locals in the Little Western Bar. (From a hotel brochure)

Come to our restaurant where good food is an unexpected pleasure. We have a large dining area where parties of up to 100 can and have been done. (From a restaurant advertisement)

> **If all be true that I do think**
> **There are five reasons we should**
> **drink;**
> **Good wine, a friend, or being dry**
> **Or lest we should be, by and by,**
> **Or any other reason why.**
> Dr Henry Aldrich

Garlic has a very short freezer life. Better to add it after thawing.

Nouvelle Cuisine

Although it is thought to have had its day, there are many who will mourn the passing of *nouvelle cuisine*, for this style of cooking added a new meaning to eating out.

No more plates laden with vast quantities of food followed by a night of indigestion; no more food swimming in basic white sauce with different flavouring and colourings; and no more overcooked vegetables ladled enthusiastically onto your already-brimming plate, whether or not you wanted them.

Instead, small (some say too small) portions of lightly cooked, delicately flavoured food were perched on a small pool of colourful and wonderfully tasty coulis or sauce, with a few tiny bits and pieces of garnish, all arranged to resemble a picture on a plate.

Wonderful for those on a diet, and for those having to eat out for business purposes several times a week, but perhaps not quite so wonderful for the working farmer or the plain greedy, and a disaster for those who failed to appreciate that they were paying for quality not quantity.

There is good news, though, for all the wives who have watched their starving husbands perching uncomfortably on the edge of dainty chairs in an elegant restaurant, trying to make two small slices of meat last as long as a steak. Most *nouvelle cuisine* restaurants have seen the light and now serve sensible portions of the same delicious food, so there should be no need to fill up on cheese on toast on returning home.

Long live the duck breasts, warm salads and raspberry vinegar beloved by *nouvelle cuisine*!

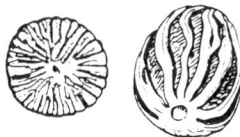

Nutmeg

Nutmeg and its similarly-flavoured companion, mace, both come from the nutmeg tree: nutmeg is the fruit, and mace its outer sheath. Nutmeg will stay fresh indefinitely and can be grated as needed. It adds an interesting flavour to white sauces, mashed potatoes, fish dishes, cakes and puddings.

Nutrition   Nowadays the British are a thoroughly vitamin-conscious lot. But it was not until the late 19th century that vitamins were considered necessary to good health.

Among the town-dwelling poor of the time rickets and scurvy were commonplace. In the country, however, people were able to trap rabbits, grow their own vegetables, produce eggs, and consequently tended to eat better than their city counterparts.

When conscription was introduced in 1916, the military authorities were horrified to discover the extent of undernourishment throughout the country. Over one million men out of two-and-a-half million who were given a medical examination were found to be unfit for military service. The government therefore decided that, to raise the overall standard of diet, they would take over the handling of the more essential foodstuffs and control prices so that they became affordable to working people.

In 1931 subsidised milk in schools helped both children and farmers, who had difficulty selling their products because of the Depression.

When war broke out in 1939 the nutritionists realised that while rationing was inevitable, what food there was available would be so packed full of vitamins and minerals that everyone would have the necessary nutrition.

The food habits of the nation have changed so much since the two world wars that malnutrition has been almost wiped out. But the advances have brought problems. With the emergence of packaged convenience foods, frozen foods and home freezing, the joys of overeating and obesity have replaced the miseries of hunger, in the West at any rate.

One cup of raw rice yields three cups of cooked rice.

Old English   During the medieval period there was little difference throughout
Cuisine   all Europe in what people ate. The aristocracy had kitchens in their homes and could afford to eat well. The poor ate whatever produce they could grow, catch or poach.

In the 16th and 17th centuries, however, national and regional styles started to develop. The English became noted for the amount of meat consumed – not in stews or casseroles but as whole joints, generally roasted. Beef, mutton, pork, fowl, rabbits and pigeon were served in large quantities. Vegetables were not popular and this excess of meat and lack of greens led to a deficiency of Vitamin A – a cause of weak eyesight.

In 1660 a French visitor to England wrote, 'The English are not very dainty, and the greatest lords' tables (who do not keep French cooks) are covered only with large dishes of meat.'

The French had introduced garnishes to their cookery, but this did not catch on in England. In the 17th century Puritanism had a strong influence. Herbs and spices were banned as they contributed, it was alleged, to licentiousness and lust, and the celebrational feasts of Christmas and other holidays were abolished.

In 1872, a German visitor wrote of his landlady's meal that 'An English dinner generally consists of a piece of half-boiled or half-roasted meat, and a few cabbage leaves boiled in plain water, on which they pour a sauce made of flour and butter.' Potatoes were served as one of normally two vegetables – both of which were boiled. Definitely the days of meat & two veg.

St. Thomas Onions

Onions

*There is in every cook's opinion
No savoury dish without an onion;
But lest your cooking should be spoiled
The onion must be thoroughly boiled.*
Jonathan Swift

In ancient Egypt the onion was considered divine, its layers symbolising the nature of the universe. Since then this essential vegetable has been incorporated into almost every country's cookery. In folklore it has its place too, being said to cure toothache, baldness, rabies and insomnia.

The onion is of the same family as chives, garlic and shallots – all of which are anti-social to some degree. But only the onion makes the cook cry, due to sulphur compounds in its oils which are released when the vegetable is cut.

O Oregano

Oregano   A herb much used in Mediterranean countries, it is delicious with tomatoes and tomato sauces – therefore a natural with pasta and pizza.

Oregano is also sometimes known as wild marjoram.

Oysters

> 'A loaf of bread,' the Walrus said,
> 'Is what we chiefly need:
> Pepper and vinegar besides
> Are very good indeed –
> Now, if you're ready, Oysters dear,
> We can begin to feed.'
> But answer there came none –
> And this was scarcely odd because
> They'd eaten every one.
> Lewis Carroll

It was a very brave man who first ate an oyster. Who would have thought that the grey blob in the middle of that tough, sharp shell would be edible? And if that first oyster eaten was also a little old, then he was very likely the first gourmet to discover food poisoning – and food poisoning from shellfish is a never-to-be-forgotten experience.

However, the oyster is worth the risk, and England produces some of the best. The historian, Sallust, in about 50 BC wrote, 'The poor Britons, there is some good to them after all – they produce an oyster.'

To cook oysters is to spoil them. Champagne slips nicely down with a dozen or so served in the shell on a bed of ice, with a little cayenne pepper and tabasco sauce.

P's and Q's   This phrase, meaning to behave oneself, probably originated in the taverns when it was legal for customers to drink on credit.

There was often a board in the bar on which the landlord would note down whether his customers drank pints or quarts. If the drinker became a little too merry he would be told to 'mind his P's and Q's'.

When he had settled his bill he would have 'wiped the slate clean', and when he started again it was 'with a clean slate'.

Parsley   Parsley was introduced to Britain in the mid 16th century and, with sage, is among the most widely used of all herbs. As a garnish it appears on just about everything, and if the phrase 'Oh, parsley' is said with enough vehemence, it doubles as an expletive in polite company.

Because parsley keeps green for so long, the ancient Greeks decked tombs with it. In French it is called *persil* ... which looks very curious on menus.

Parson   One of the great classic diaries is that of Parson Woodforde – the
Woodforde Revd. James Woodforde who, in the second half of the 18th century,
               was Vicar of Weston Longville in Norfolk. His vast and fascinating
               diary of country life paid particular attention to food and drink.

*The first course was part of a large
Cod, a Chine of Mutton, some
soup, a Chicken Pye, Puddings and
Roasts etc. Second course,
Pidgeons and Asparagus. A Fillet of
Veal with Mushrooms and high
sauce with it, roasted Sweetbread,
hot Lobster, Apricot Tart, and in the
middle a Pyramid of Syllabubs and
Jellies. We had dessert of Fruit after
dinner and Madeira, white Port
and red to drink as wine. We were
very cheerful and merry.*

Gout, not surprisingly, was very common then.

P Pears

Pears   Homer called them 'gifts of the gods', and they have been cultivated for over 3000 years. They were sacred to Venus and regarded both as an aphrodisiac and as a medicine. In middle Europe it was said that, if one dreamt of pears, riches and happiness would come, and if a woman dreamt of them she would marry above her station.

There are literally thousands of varieties, but the best known are Comice – the juiciest; Conference – harder, but good for cooking; and Williams – an English variety called Bartlett in America.

Use scissors to cut herbs for garnish.

Peas   The humble pea is probably the only vegetable which does not deteriorate in its frozen state. The most popular variety, the *petit pois*, is wonderful from the packets available in supermarkets – unlike most other frozen products.

In general, however, the cooking lacks something. As William Wallace Irwin put it:

> *In the vegetable world, there is nothing so innocent, so confiding in its expression, as the small green face of the freshly-shelled spring pea. Asparagus is pushing and bossy, lettuce is loud and blowsy, radishes are gay and playful, but the little green pea is so helpless and friendly that it makes really sensitive stomachs suffer to see how he is treated in the average home. Fling him into the water and let him boil – and that's that.*

For a change, a sophisticated treatment is *Petit Pois à la Francaise. Sauté a little onion and shredded lettuce in butter, cover with water and bring to the boil. Add salt, a dash of brown sugar, mint if you have it and the peas. Simmer until the peas are tender. Drain and serve.*

According to legend, peas came from the Garden of Eden, and remains more than 5,000 years old have been found in a Bronze Age settlement. These are clearly of the very same variety as used in many cafés and pubs, which also seem to be made of bronze.

Canned peas are dried peas which have been soaked and cooked before canning. Mushy peas from the North of England are processed peas as well, and do not bear thinking about.

Pepper   Wonderful stuff.

As with brown sugar, most dishes benefit from the addition of a little pepper. It is both a stimulant and an aid to digestion and is, after salt, the most widely used of all condiments.

Peppercorns exist in three different colours – black, white and green – and are the dried berries of the pepper vine picked at different stages of maturity.

The insatiable demand for pepper, amongst other delicacies, led to the discovery by Vasco da Gama in 1498 of the sea route from Europe to India. The Venetians and Genoese held a monopoly on pepper. It was transported overland to Europe by caravan and ship, which made it so expensive that it was sometimes used for bartering when precious metals were scarce.

It is, of course, the famous ingredient of the *au poivre* sauce which, of all sauces, is probably the most widely mis-made. It must be made with whole crushed peppercorns which are pressed into the meat before cooking. The sauce is made from the juice of the meat, brandy, cream and butter.

If you ever come across it on a restaurant menu, try ice cream *au poivre* – which is only vanilla ice cream with ground black pepper, and much better-tasting than it sounds.

Picnics   Terribly English in spite of the weather – and uninvited insect guests.

Marie Dressler summed it up: 'If ants are such busy workers, how come they find time to go to all the picnics?'

> *An egg is always an adventure. It may be different.*
> Oscar Wilde.

Pimms   In the 1880s James Pimm opened an oyster bar in the City of London and became famous for the gin slings he concocted there. His successors capitalised on that success and bottled his concoctions for sale to bars and restaurants.

Ever since, the bright young things only acknowledge the beginning of summer by drinking the first Pimms.

Though the recipe is secret, a very good imitation can be made by mixing one-third vermouth to two-thirds gin and, when topped up with lemonade (or half lemonade and soda), a lot of ice, a slice of lemon and some cucumber peel, it is difficult to spot the difference. Purists add mint and /or borage, and the whole is best made in large glass jugs to save the trouble of getting up to make refills.

At one time gin, rum, brandy and vodka-based Pimms were available, but these have almost disappeared, and the most widely available variation now is gin-based. In bars they have the habit of turning a Pimms into a mildly alcoholic fruit salad.

> *Food is an important part of a balanced diet.*
> Fran Lebowitz

Plonk
Today this means cheap wine of any sort. This is possibly a First World War soldier's version of the French word for white wine, *blanc,* though Godfrey Smith in *The English Companion* says that it was, quite simply, rhyming slang for *vin blanc* – plinkety-plonk.

Ploughman's Lunch
The traditional meal of good crusty bread, farmhouse cheese and pickled onions has been enjoyed by the English for generations and generations, stretching back to the early 1970s when the English County Cheese Council unmasked the term 'Ploughman's Lunch' as an advertising slogan.

The innkeepers of those early days adapted the idea, and now one can have a slab of mass-produced bread, plastic cheese, individually-wrapped portions of butter substitute and ball-bearings masquerading as pickled onions for a sum that gives the owner only about a thousand per cent profit.

Potato Crisps
The story goes that the invention of the potato crisp is credited to an American who, whilst staying in a fashionable holiday resort in New York state in 1865, never stopped complaining. He seemed to find fault with everything. He even grumbled that the French fries served with his meal were soggy and much too greasy.

The complaint was passed to the cook who, because the guest was so miserable, thought he might succeed where everyone else had failed by preparing for him something really special. This time he sliced the potatoes extremely thinly and deep fried them.

The result was a completely new product with which even the disgruntled guest could find no fault. Indeed he went so far as to admit that he had never tasted anything so delicious.

Such was his pleasure that he spread the news of this delectable new product far and wide, and that is how the potato crisp came about – all because of one man who had a chip on his shoulder.

Wash strawberries before hulling them or they will absorb water.

Punch   Probably the name stems from the time when the British ruled India and would make for themselves a drink of five ingredients – tea, water, sugar, lemon juice and the local spirit – so blended that no one flavour was predominant. The Hindu word for five is *panch*.

In an 1869 book, *Cooling Cups and Dainty Drinks*, William Terrington quoted the following:

> **Whene'er a bowl of punch**
> **we make**
> **Four striking opposites we take –**
> **The strong, the small, the sharp,**
> **the sweet,**
> **Together mixed, most kindly meet.**
> **And when they happily unite**
> **The bowl is 'fragant with delight'.**

A Caribbean recipe calls for a mixture of 'one of sour, two of sweet, three of strong and four of weak'.

In 1746, 6000 guests were entertained by the Commander in Chief of the British Forces with a punch made from 250 gallons of brandy, 25,000 lemons, 20 gallons of lime juice, 1300 lbs sugar, 5 lbs nutmeg and 105 gallons of white wine. It was placed in a marble fountain and served by a succession of ship's boys, who had to be replaced when they were overcome by the alcohol fumes.

There are non-alcoholic punches which are excellent for parties, hot punches for cold nights and the mild punch of the 18th century which consisted of one part milk, one part brandy and one part rum. Beaten eggs, spices, sugar and lemon were added, but did little to dilute a very potent mixture.

Pussyfoot   A term for non-alcoholic drinks and punches. The name stems from W. E. (Pussyfoot) Johnson, a temperance advocate in America during the beginning of this century who gained his nickname from his 'catlike' pursual of lawbreakers in gambling saloons in Indian territories, when he was serving as Chief Special Officer of the US Indian Service.

Q Quail

Upon retirement he devoted his energies to lecturing (over 4000 times) on temperance and prohibition. In 1919, Mr 'Pussyfoot' Johnson appeared in Britain to join the anti-drink campaigners. *The Times* reported that he was eventually routed by the united medical student population of London, who seized him during a public debate and submitted him to various indignities, including sousing him with a large bottle of Bass.

There are many good recipes for pussyfoot punches. Normally fruit-based, with the addition of some of the non-alcoholic wines, angostura bitters, concentrated cordials and sparkling water or soda, they look interesting, taste good and please anyone who wants to avoid alcohol.

Grow basil on the kitchen windowsill in pots to keep flies away.

Quail

Legend has it that the quail is of an inordinately amorous disposition, and in early Elizabethan times its name was given as a slang term to Courtesans. It is the smallest of game birds, and belongs to the same family as pheasant and partridge.

In Great Britain quails have become very rare, and the birds and their eggs are protected.

They're very difficult to eat – full of bones – and not really a very satisfying meal. The effort of eating one is scarcely repaid by the taste. However, *nouvelle cuisine* restaurants have instead introduced quail eggs which do have an exceptionally strong taste to them.

Quiche Lorraine

As the name implies, quiche comes from Lorraine in France, each region of Lorraine having its own type.

The quiche is much beloved of pubs and delicatessens – it's cheap to make or buy, and can be sold at a good profit. All too often they are soggy, heavy slices of a custardy egg mix. Some places will serve them hot – after placing them in the microwave oven to ensure the total removal of any taste. Garnished with a huge mound of chips they are truly disgusting.

Quince

A real quince is seldom seen today, though at one time it was grown with apple and pear trees, to whose family it belongs. It looks like a cross between the two – yellow in colour and with a downy skin. It was thought by some to have been the forbidden fruit and it was the Greeks' 'golden apple' of legend.

The trees flourish in Portugal and their name for the quince is *marmelo,* a possible source for the word 'marmalade'.

Quince can only be eaten cooked and is most usually made into jelly or a preserve with another fruit.

The ornamental variety is the well-known Japonica, and if the 'apples' from this bush are collected in the autumn they can be made into a delicious pink jelly which goes very well with lamb and game, as a change from redcurrant.

Rabbit Man

Rabbits Rabbits were introduced into Britain by the Romans who bred them in special gardens attached to their villas. Though they escaped into the wild and bred prolifically, they were unable to survive in the forests because of the foxes and other carnivores. Reintroduced by the Norman invaders, rabbits eventually gained a strong ecological foothold.

By the 17th and 18th centuries, rabbits were a staple fare of the country folk, and an old country rhyme records:

For rabbits young and rabbits old,
For rabbits hot and rabbits cold,
For rabbits tender and rabbits tough,
We thank thee Lord, we've had enough.

Wild rabbit may be unpalatable but much of the rabbit eaten today has been bred specially for the table, and has a whiter and eminently more digestable flesh than wild rabbits.

R Raisins

> *Cauliflower is nothing but cabbage*
> *with a college education.*
> Mark Twain

Raisins   Raisins are merely dried grapes which, until the middle of the 19th century, came from Spain, Greece or Turkey. The vines were planted in California in the 1850s, and that state is now the world's largest producer – followed by Australia, South Africa and Afghanistan.

A currant is the smallest dried grape; muscatels are very large, juicy, sun-dried raisins from Spain; and sultanas come from a seedless white grape, also dried.

Those dried grapes found lurking in every bowl of muesli will almost certainly be currants – they're far cheaper than raisins and sultanas. But raisins, with the highest sugar content, provide the most concentrated energy source.

Boil water with half a lemon to remove dark stains on aluminium saucepans.

Restaurant   Some restaurant menus deserve a prize for literary merit. Usually the
Menus – a   size of a newspaper and overly ornate, they include descriptive
Layman's   passages too florid even for Mills and Boon readers to digest. With
Guide   a little practice one can read between the lines and get a fair idea of what is actually on offer.

'Luscious Atlantic shellfish on a bed of crisp green lettuce enlivened with a traditional sauce of blended tomato, mayonnaise and herbs' is, in reality, a prawn cocktail with bottled Marie Rose sauce.

The 'prime pieces of beef from the best of British cattle, lovingly marinated in red Burgundy to bring out their piquant flavour, and served with the finest of spring vegetables' turns out to be a rather ordinary stew.

One extremely good profit-earner is the 'tender slivers of prime fillet of beef sautéd with mushrooms and cream'. The leftover trimmings of the fillet which cannot be served as steaks are here turned into Beef Strogonoff and offered at an exorbitant price.

The tough old piece of battery hen is described as 'corn-fed, farm-fresh, lovingly-reared chicken'.

For 'mushrooms hand-picked in the dew-fresh morning in the garden of England' read 'cultivated mushrooms which have probably been in the fridge for a week'.

If you desire the 'mélange of exotic flavours and tastes from around the world served with an original ice cream of your choice', expect fruit salad.

'Dairy fresh' means dairy frozen, and 'homemade' is from a very large factory in the heart of industrial England.

The 'piquant sauce' is bottled.

'Sea fresh' is frozen in bright orange breadcrumbs, and the side salad you get bears no relation to the 'symphony of harmonious vegetables', 'enhanced' or 'lacquered' or 'moistened' with a 'subtle blend of fine herbs and oil'.

Restaurants – Past

In the 18th century the only places where people could eat were the inns, which served fixed meals at fixed times, and the shops of the *traiteurs* (eating-house keepers) who had a monopoly on the sale of cooked foods.

In 1765 a man called Boulanger opened a shop in Paris selling fortifying soups. Above the door he advertised (in Latin) ; 'Come to me, you whose stomach labours, and I will restore you', and he gave to his soups the name *restaurantis,* or restoratives.

Wishing to expand his menu, Boulanger began to offer his customers sheeps' feet in white wine. Furious at seeing their monopoly threatened, the 'corporation of traiteurs' brought a law suit against him which, after a long battle, he won. The resultant publicity made Parisian society rush to his restaurant to try this dish.

R **Restaurants – Present**

Other restaurants soon followed and expanded the choices available to their – generally rich – guests. Then, thanks to the French Revolution, restaurants became popular as meeting places, multiplied and were open to all citizens, irrespective of wealth. From that time on, the habit of eating out was no longer the privilege of the rich.

After the French Revolution English visitors rediscovered France and found there over 500 restaurants of good quality. The idea was brought back to England and the first restaurants were built as part of larger hotels, often at railway stations such as Charing Cross.

With huge French menus they were very popular with the middle and upper classes, who realised that eating out could be fun if creature comforts were not lacking.

**Restaurants
– Present**
All too often a restaurant today is a place where the proprietor tries to separate as much money from as many people as possible, by giving them as little enjoyment and as much discomfort as can be arranged.

A few general rules for eaters-out are:

- Don't patronise a place where you can't see what you're eating. The cool, dark alcoves and rooms probably hide an inch-thick coating of dust and the gloom will obscure a multitude of sins on your plate!

- If the menu is large and engraved and it takes an hour to read it all, the food is going to come out of the freezer and into the microwave. Huge menus cannot be run unless it's the Dorchester.

- If the prices look reasonable, check to see if they include vegetables. You can easily run up an extra £3 or £4 per head with all the extras.

- When you've ordered a particularly good bottle of wine, watch the waiter open it. Discourage the dreadful habit of the bottle being whisked away and kept by the wine waiter. He is probably helping himself to your wine!

Rhubarb
Rhubarb reached Europe sometime in the 14th century, having found its way here from Northern Asia. As the first of the spring produce it was traditionally eaten to cleanse the system of the winter stodge: hence its reputation as a purgative.

It is, strictly speaking, a vegetable – it is the stalk that is the edible part. The leaves should not be eaten as they contain oxalic acid which is a poison. In his *Devil's Dictionary* Ambrose Bierce refers to it as 'vegetable essence of stomach ache'.

To clean a stained or blackened saucepan, cook rhubarb in it – but don't eat the rhubarb!

Rhyming Slang

"

I felt like a gay and frisky, or even a bit of the in and out before I had my Lilley and Skinner of Kate and Sydney, Rosebuds, Uncle Fred followed by a bit of give and take. Thence to the rubbidy dub for an evening of Vera Lynn and Apple Fritter, knowing when I returned I would be in a very hot fisherman's daughter.

"

In other words:

"

I decided to have a whisky or a stout before I partook of my dinner of steak and kidney, potatoes, bread and a bit of cake. Afterwards to the pub for an evening on gin and bitter, fully aware that when I got home I would be in very hot water.

"

Ritz, Cesar   'Public schools are open to all – like the Ritz', a political wag once observed.

César Ritz would have approved of that observation. He brought hotel-keeping in Europe to a fine art at the turn of this century, and gave his name to the two superlative establishments which still flourish in London and Paris.

It was in Monte Carlo that Ritz met Escoffier, the famous chef, who inspired in him a yearning for excellence. He acquired a controlling interest in a hotel in Cannes, began making changes when the Prince of Wales (later Edward VII) came to stay, and the name of Ritz became synonymous with quality.

R Rosemary

When Ritz came to London in 1898 to view the Savoy Hotel, he realised that in England there was a clientele ready to pay any price in order to have the best. Escoffier was persuaded to come with him, and within a very short time the Savoy was considered the best hotel in Britain. It was the place to be seen: its patrons included stars of the theatre, famous singers, famous beauties and royalty.

Together, Ritz and Escoffier set the standard for the hotel industry that was to follow.

The Savoy was the first hotel to have a bathroom for each room. Music whilst you dined was introduced, and Johann Strauss was once employed to conduct the Savoy orchestra.

Ritz planned a series of grand hotels all over Europe, the finest of which was in Paris; he also had plans for Ritz hotels in New York, Madrid, Cairo and, of course, the famous Ritz hotel in Piccadilly which opened in 1905.

The name has now passed into colloquial usage to describe anything fashionable and very luxurious.

To keep a sauce warm, or to reheat it, place pan in which it is made into a larger one of gently-simmering water to provide all-round heat.

Rosemary   Of Mediterranean origin, rosemary is one of the strongest and most distinctive herbs. The Italians are particularly fond of it – along with garlic – and it has always been associated with remembrance and fidelity.

The name comes from the Latin *ros marinus* which means 'sea dew', and as Venus – the love goddess – sprang from the foam of the sea, rosemary or sea dew is said to have amatory qualities.

According to Culpepper, the herbalist, 'it quickens a weak memory and the senses'. At one time, it was extensively taken as a nerve tonic.

In Europe, rosemary is often worn at marriages and funerals. It contains tannin, resin and an essential oil which is used in perfumes and cosmetics. It was believed in the Middle Ages to ward off every-thing from evil spirits to the bubonic plague.

Rump and Dozen   'A rump of beef and a dozen of Claret' was a not-uncommon wager amongst sportsmen of the late 18th and early 19th centuries.

It can also mean a rump steak and a dozen oysters, though they make an uneasy partnership.

Rye   Rye is a cereal which is closely related to wheat. It is often used to make
                rye bread which, because of its rather powerful flavour, was never
                favoured in Britain but has always been very popular in Europe.

                The Scandinavians are particularly fond of rye bread, and often use
                it as the base for Danish open sandwiches.

                Many crispbreads and crunchy biscuits are also made from rye flour.

                But perhaps it is best used to make rye whisky – so nice to get one's
                roughage in a glass!

> **Rise at five, dine at nine, sup at five,
> to bed at nine.**
> Rabelais

Saffron   Naturalised in Britain now (Edward VI's Secretary of State introduced
                it to Saffron Walden in Essex in the mid-15th century), this spice from
                the autumn crocus still brings a touch of the exotic East to the kitchen.

                It is estimated that 75,000 hand-picked blossoms are needed to
                produce 1 lb of saffron, one acre yielding only 12 lbs. So it is very
                expensive.

                Use sparingly. With rice, a touch of modestly-priced turmeric serves
                the same colouring purpose.

Sage   Sage is one of the commonest of kitchen herbs. Yet how many cooks
                realise that it grows in more than 750 varieties? It has been called 'the
                herb of Jupiter' and, because it was believed that it promoted long
                life, 'Sage the Saviour'.

                Before the invention of toothpaste, sage leaves were rubbed over the
                teeth to whiten them.

                But it remains, for most people, the essential ingredient for a good
                tangy stuffing . . . An idea, clearly, much in the mind of the American
                statesman and lawyer William Maxwell Evarts when he rose at a
                Thanksgiving dinner and said, 'You have been giving your attention
                to a turkey stuffed with sage; you are now about to consider a sage
                stuffed with turkey.'

Saint Martin The patron saint of innkeepers is also the patron saint of reformed
                drunkards. Presumably the two are somehow related. He was born
                a heathen but converted to Catholicism and became Bishop of Tours
                in 371.

                His day is November 11, which is also the date of the pagan Feast of
                Bacchus, god of wine – which cheerful coincidence no doubt led to
                his bibulous patronage. He was renowned for his good works, selfless
                generosity and miracles. So raise a glass in his honour . . .

Saint's Day Feasts   Hundreds of saints are recognised these days – so many that only a small proportion can be given a day to themselves. Those that are commemorated with a 'Saint's Day' are often associated with some special feast or food.

St Valentine's Day (14 February) is associated with sweets and chocolate or heart-shaped cakes. No-one really knows why – St Valentine was a Roman priest clubbed to death for his religious beliefs in the third century AD.

St David's Day (1 March) remembers the patron saint of Wales, and a stew of beef with chopped parsnips, turnips, onions, carrots, potatoes and plenty of leeks is served. This is called *cawl*.

The Irish have St Patrick's Day (17 March), and at one time innkeepers would provide 'Patrick's Pot' (beer or whiskey – Irish, of course) for their customers, and serve bread and fish.

In England, 23 April is St George's Day – when you can have nothing better than good English beef and Yorkshire pudding.

St Andrew's Day (30 November) is celebrated by all right-thinking Scots with haggis and copious draughts of whisky . . . along with Burns Night, New Year's Eve and any other excuse they can think of.

Salad as Art   The British landscape painter, Joseph Turner, was handed a salad at his table one day.

Turner looked at it and remarked to his neighbour, 'Nice cool green that lettuce, isn't it? And the beetroot pretty red – not quite strong enough; and the mixture, delicate tint of yellow that. Add some mustard, and then you have one of my pictures.'

> **Great food is like great sex – the more you have the more you want.**
> Gail Green

Salad Dressing   According to a Spanish proverb, four persons are needed to make a good salad dressing – a spendthrift for oil, a miser for vinegar, a counsellor for salt and a madman to stir it all up.

Salmon   The king of fish deserves treatment worthy of it. It is all too often over-cooked and served up as an unappetising lump.

Cook it whole in a fish kettle, just covered with water to which some wine, lemon slices, peppercorns, salt and onion have been added.

Bring to the boil and *immediately* it begins to bubble take it off the heat and let it cool in its water until quite cold.

It is then perfectly cooked.

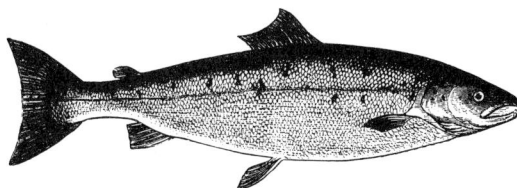

Salt   Salt (sodium chloride) is the only mineral condiment that is added to a meal. It is essential to human life, as it regulates the body fluids, and it is one of the oldest methods of preserving food.

It is present in meat, fish, milk and eggs but there is very little in fruit and vegetables, so vegetarians should include extra salt in their diet.

The ancient Romans often served out rations of salt and other necessities to their soldiers and court servants. These rations were known by the general term *sal* (salt), and when money was substituted for these rations it was called *sal-arium* (salary).

To 'eat a man's salt' means to partake of his hospitality. The Arabs take this a step further: eating a man's salt creates a sacred bond between host and guest.

Tomatoes will peel more easily if boiling water is poured over them and they are left to stand for a few minutes.

S Sandwich

Sandwich   Although the principle of the sandwich was known in Roman times, history has credited John Montagu, Fourth Earl of Sandwich, with instructing his servant to put some beef between two slabs of bread so he could eat without interrupting his card game.

Montagu's family tried to tidy up the reason for his invention by insisting that the pressing nature of affairs of State caused him to create the snack – but the gambling-house version is confirmed by 'reliable sources'.

Too often these days sandwiches are still a slice of unpalatable something slapped between two wedges of bread with nothing else but margarine.

Lettuce, parsley, celery and the like will keep fresh for a week if wrapped in a wet cloth, kept damp and stored in the refrigerator or another cool place.

Sauce   One might be forgiven for thinking that all graduates from catering colleges are taught that the basic rule of saucing is 'If it doesn't move, slap a white sauce on it.'

It is so easy for a kitchen to have a big pot of sauce ready for everything – and can be very useful for concealing a multitude of sins.

J.R. Lowell, the American poet and essayist, put his finger on it (or in it) when he wrote in his *Biglow Papers:*

> **Of all the sarse that I can call to mind, England doos the most unpleasant kind.**

Bottles of tomato sauce and mint sauce tend to be placed on the family table with salad dressing – and all are quite often put on the plate together.

Since bought sauces taste more of vinegar than anything else, maybe the bottles are there to provide diners with something to read at the table – to save the embarrassment of actually having to talk to each other.

Scampi   Scampi are small crustacea of the lobster family. Just to confuse things, the French call them *langoustines* and the British often call them Dublin Bay Prawns – though they're neither prawns nor found in Dublin Bay.

Scampi was introduced to the British public in the 1950s when a West End restaurant which had ordered lobster received scampi instead. The chef that day prepared the first of millions upon millions of deep-fried portions of them.

The tasteless stuff you get in pubs and many restaurants in that bright orange covering bears no relation to real scampi. Unless you're desperate for sustenance, ignore it.

Scones

It appears that scones are making a comeback. Fed up with croissants and muffins, the British now yearn for the gentler days of afternoon tea with fresh scones, served hot with real strawberry jam and dollops of thick cream.

Any establishment which serves scones properly deserves to be declared a national treasure. The old English tearoom is one of the last bastions of civilisation in this age of prepackaged and processed fast food. At home they're made quickly and easily – no need at all for ghastly packet mixes.

Vegetarianism is harmless enough, though it is apt to fill a man with wind and self-righteousness.
Sir Robert Hutchinson

Scottish Cuisine

Scotland has close ties with the Nordic countries which, in the Viking days of rape and pillage, passed on (when time permitted) methods of salting and curing.

The country's food has its own peculiar identity, from porridge to haggis. Dr Johnson observed: 'If an epicure could remove by a wish in quest of sensual gratification, wherever he had supped, he would breakfast in Scotland.'

Scotland is famed for its shortbreads, Dundee cakes, Scotch Broth and Cock-a-leekie. Forfar bridies are the Scottish equivalent of Cornish pasties. *Howtowdie wi'drappit eggs* is a chicken dish steamed with onions and potatoes, and served with poached eggs. The salmon is superb.

And then, of course, there is haggis – which is very good, but one has to admit, an acquired taste.

Hogmanay, Scotland's celebration of the last day of the year, has been exported to England and now features each New Year's Eve on television. Traditionally the fortunes of the household are determined by the first person to cross the threshold after midnight. This should be a dark man – not a member of the family – who brings with him bread, salt and coal – symbols of life, hospitality and warmth.

S Sirloin of Beef

Sirloin of Beef

Stories abound about an English King (Henry VIII, James I, Charles II – sources disagree as to which one) who was so pleased with a cut of meat he was given that he knighted it 'Sir Loin.'

The truth is more mundane. It is a corruption of the French *sur loin* – 'above' or 'on' the loin.

James I is recorded as saying at a banquet, 'Bring hither that surloin, sirrah, for 'tis worthy of a more honourable post, being, as I may say, not "sur" loin but "sir" loin.'

Never double salt if you double quantities. Add the single amount and taste.

Smokers

Whilst reasonable souls will say that everyone has the right to go to hell in the manner of their own choosing, that doesn't mean that they have the right to take others along for the ride. Evidence is strong enough to show that this is what smokers do.

Even worse than inhaling second-hand smoke, however, is the ruination of good food and drink that occurs when wafts of smoke drift across the plate and nestle in the glass. Possibly smoking should be restricted – if only as a matter of common courtesy – to a time when diners have finished eating?

There are also some smokers who could usefully bear in mind that ashtrays are for ash, coffee cups for coffee and butter dishes for butter – and remember that cigarette stubs belong only in the first of these receptacles . . .

Smorgasbord From Sweden, Smorgasbord now means an enormous buffet of hot and cold dishes, but was originally designed just as an *hors d'oeuvre*.

It should start with a variety of cold herring dishes, followed by cold fish, meat and salads and finish with a selection of hot dishes – mainly roast meats and often including reindeer meat.

Smorgasbords are wonderful for guaranteed indigestion – it is impossible not to overeat.

Perhaps the Swedes should consider offering 'bed and smorgasbord'?

> *No man can be wise on an empty stomach.*
> *George Eliot*

Snails Irwin Shaw was once kept waiting in a restaurant. When the *maitre d'hotel* finally approached him, he was informed that snails were the speciality of the house. 'I know', he replied. 'And you've got them dressed as waiters.'

Snails have been eaten since prehistoric times, when the art of fattening them by feeding them on herbs, wine and spicy food first evolved. In the 17th and 18th centuries, snail soup was popular for curing chest problems.

To avoid the risk of poisoning, snails are steamed for some time before they are cooked and eaten, as they may have eaten plants harmless to them but poisonous to man.

In Gloucestershire and Somerset they are called wallfish – presumably because of their climbing abilities. In Catholic countries they are popular on meatless days as they are not considered to be meat.

S Soya

Soya   One of the major crops of the world, probably originally from China, the soya plant has the merit of being free from attack from insect pests and it grows easily in dry countries.

Vegetarians love it and take great delight in serving up this unpalatable vegetable to non-vegetarian friends.

As Fran Lebowitz so eloquently put it:

> *Inhabitants of underdeveloped nations and victims of natural disasters are the only people who have ever been happy to see soya beans.*

Soyer, Alexis   As an exasperated journalist of the early 19th century wrote:

> *The British people have done mighty things in the course of their history. They have created a vast empire and established a greater Britain at the antipodes; they have practically invented the steam engine and railroads, actually invented penny postage, but they have never as a nation been able to make omelettes properly, and never will do so.'*

Influenced by comments such as these, a French cook named Alexis Soyer arrived in England in 1830 with the aim of revolutionising the country's cookery and civilising the barbarous culinary customs of the natives.

His debut in London was as *Chef de Cuisine* at the Reform Club and, though his dinners and banquets became the talk of the town, he was not content to cater for aristocratic society alone.

Soyer's dream was to reform the cooking of the whole country, and he wrote cookbooks for every market he could find. There was *A Gastronomic Regenerator* for gourmets; a collection of recipes for the middle classes and the modern housewife; and his still-famous *Shilling Cookery* for the people – full of nutritious, wholesome, quickly and economically-prepared recipes.

Soyer also invented a simple 'magic' stove which could be placed, so the advertisement said, 'in the parlour of the wealthy, the studio of the artist, and the attic of the humble'. He was dubbed by both press and public 'the only true Minister of the Interior' and 'Emperor of the Kitchen'.

When the great Crystal Palace exhibition was held in 1851, Soyer set up a restaurant nearby. In its own way it was as imposing and as impressive as the Crystal Palace itself. No expense was spared with the building and apartments decorated sumptuously according to the Arabian Nights. Five to six thousand guests were to be entertained daily. Although everyone was at first eager to inspect this astonishing place, few cared to visit a second time once the novelty had worn off. Expenses kept rising, and eventually – almost broke – Soyer had to close the place down.

Although this was a bitter blow, it didn't daunt him. Three years later, Soyer offered to go out to the battlefront of the Crimean War, at his own expense, and devote himself to the reformation of the kitchen in war. Scandalised by the conditions he found there, he opened new kitchens, set up bakeries, devised nourishing menus and trained cooks. He was referred to at the time as the male parallel of Miss Nightingale, and *Punch* declared him worthy of 'an earldom at least for solacing and strengthening the vitals of the whole army'.

But Soyer returned to England exhausted, and sick with Crimean fever. He died in 1858.

Line your grill pans with foil to save having to clean them every time.

Spritzer   In the summer, a refreshing long drink of white wine and soda (or sometimes sparkling mineral water). It evolved from the hock and seltzer that was very popular in the last century.

The spritzer is still causing confusion in some pubs:

Customer to barman:
Could I have a spritzer please?
Barman:
Sorry, lady, don't stock that.
Customer:
I'll have a white wine and soda then.
Barman:
Certainly!

S Spuds

When the recipe says a pinch, it is usually ⅛ teaspoon.

Spuds   When potatoes were first grown in England they were shunned as being very unhealthy.

It's said that food fanatics (there were some around even then) went so far as to establish a special body to warn the population of the dangers of eating these pestilential roots. They called themselves the Society for the Prevention of Undesirable and Dangerous Species . . . or SPUDS.

There is another story, however, which says that the word comes from an implement, generally used as a weeding tool, which was called a 'spudde' . . . and which came in very handy for, well, spudding up potatoes.

Steak   The word 'steak' comes from the spit on which the first slices of meat were cooked. The name of this spit – the stake – was subsequently transferred to the piece of meat itself.

> **To enjoy food and rejoice in feminine beauty is only to be human.**
> *Confucius*

Strawberries   A lady of fashion in Napoleon's day, a Madame Tallien, crushed over 20 pounds of strawberries into her bath each day to keep her skin soft as satin.

The name comes from the Anglo Saxon *streowberie,* which means 'straying plant'. Its runners stray from the parent plant in all directions.

There are those who favour pepper to bring out the flavour; the sweet-toothed dieter might try adding orange juice – no sugar should then be needed.

As Isaac Walton wrote, 'Doubtless God could have made a better berry, but doubtless God never did'.

Sugar	Sugar is extracted from many plants – cane, beet, sugar maple and some species of palm. Sucrose is cane sugar; levulose, fruit sugar; and lactose, milk sugar.

Sugar cane was probably first grown in India, and Greece and China imported it as a luxury commodity. The Persians called it 'the reed that gave honey without bees'.

In 1099 the Crusaders returned with it from Syria and in England this new spice was called 'white gold'.

With the introduction of coffee and cocoa the consumption of sugar increased in Europe, and soon Germany, France, Holland and England all had sugar refineries.

Sugar has a high calorific value, and is therefore a very concentrated-energy foodstuff which is readily absorbed. Thanks to its rapid assimilation, it restores energy very quickly – though only for a limited time, as any doctor wanting to put you on a diet will tell you.

In spite of being forbidden fruit to dieters, the word 'sugar' has also become a term of endearment. It refers as well to a young lady's elderly gentleman-friend – sugar daddy – especially one who lavishes gifts upon her, and no doubt sweetens her life considerably!

> *Cooking is like love. It should be entered into with abandon or not at all.*
> Harriet van Horne

Sunday Lunch

Sunday is normally given over to that traditional lunch which most people nowadays do not want to indulge in, but do so because they believe the rest of the family want it.

A large roast meal is produced on the one day everyone deserves to have their feet up. The family overeats and then goes to sleep in front of the T.V.

Sunday lunch out is also a much beloved custom. It means a drive in the country to a dark restaurant where the menu consists of soup of the day, roast of the day, fruit salad or apple pie and coffee, all for such a low price that it cannot be good food. Eating at its worst.

Superstitions *Unlucky 13*

'Unlucky 13' goes back to the 13 apostles, one of whom betrayed his master and hanged himself. Therefore, among 13 persons there is one who is a traitor and a potential hanged man.

This superstition applies only to those seated at a table; there is no need to worry if numbers total 13 elsewhere.

T Tabasco

If you find you have invited 13 guests to dinner, either quickly invite a fourteenth or tell one of them not to come!

Spilt salt
Salt has always been the symbol of friendship. To spill it is a sign of imminent disagreement – and bad luck. To arrest both, a few of the fallen grains should be flung over the left shoulder.

Upside-down bread
If bread, which is the staff of life, is turned upside down, it signifies death. It should never be in such a position on the table, otherwise misfortune will result.

Spilt wine
In Rome a little wine was always spilt on the table before a meal to honour the gods. It is a lucky gesture and an expression of gratitude which it is hoped will be rewarded.

A knife as a present
Any sharp, cutting or piercing instrument like a knife or scissors given as a present could cut a friendship. To avoid this, the recipient should present the giver with a small coin – thus changing the gift into a token purchase, and 'blunting' a possibly aggressive weapon.

Taking the last piece of cake
For a woman, taking the last piece of cake means a life as an old maid. It was thought that a woman who was not loath to take the last piece showed greed and selfishness, and also demonstrated traits of masculine aggressiveness which could possibly frighten off any potential suitor.

This custom may go back to biblical days where, at harvest time, the corners of a field were sometimes left unharvested for the benefit of the poor and the homeless. To take that last piece could mean an association with any of those unfortunates, which certainly spelled bad luck.

To degrease soups and stews easily, refrigerate overnight and then scoop off the solidified fat.

Tabasco

Tabasco is a tiny Mexican state from where, reputedly, chillis originally came.

The sauce which shares its name is a proprietary brand of the hottest red sauce made from those chillis. An American – Edmund McIlhenny – invented it in the 1850s. He planted some of the seeds from a handful of dried chillis a friend had brought back from Mexico. They flourished and he experimented with them, finally making a strong sauce.

Today the sauce is still made by the McIlhenny family. Used in casseroles, soups, dips etc. it adds a piquancy; added to vodka and tomato juice it peps up a Bloody Mary no end.

Use sparingly . . . unless you have an asbestos gullet.

Appetite – a universal wolf.
Shakespeare

Tablecloths Tablecloths go back to the Middle Ages when they played an
and Napkins important role in feudal ceremony.

When persons of different rank ate at the same table, the host's place alone was covered with a cloth – to set him apart from the rest of the company. If the table itself was covered, then the host's place had a second cloth over it.

Napkins as we know them now weren't used – table coverings simply had a long narrow strip laid along the edge for guests to wipe their hands and faces.

In the 16th century, table linen became fashionable and napkins were often changed with each course. They were sometimes tied around the neck of the diner to protect the fancy collars worn. This was quite a difficult operation and a guest would ask his neighbour to tie the napkin – and so was born the expression 'to make ends meet'.

T Table d'hote

Table d'hote   Literally means 'the table of the host' – the food the host is having. Travellers who agreed to eat at the host's table in early times would expect to pay less than those who ordered something special.

Nowadays the *table d'hote* menu is often compiled to use the leftovers of the previous night.

> *Thought depends absolutely on the stomach, but in spite of that, those who have the best stomachs are not the best thinkers.*
> *Voltaire*

Tapas   All Spanish bars serve these little snacks of olives, salami, tomato and anchovies to eat whilst you sip your aperitif. Originally tapas were not so appetising: they were slices of bread placed over the sherry glass to keep the flies off – the origin of Garibaldi biscuits?

Tarragon   There are two varieties of this herb – French and Russian – but only the French has any distinctive flavour. The name is derived from *dracunculus* meaning 'little dragon'.

Tarragon vinegar is easily made by placing a few sprigs of tarragon in a bottle of white wine or cider vinegar, and the herb is usually associated with béarnaise sauce, chicken dishes and fish.

It is not the gardener's favourite herb as it cannot be grown from seed, does not like hard winters, and after a few years will disappear for no apparent reason.

Tea

Tea is the most commonly-drunk of all beverages, and is made from the dried leaves of an evergreen shrub belonging to the camellia family.

Originally from China – where legend claims it was first drunk 5000 years ago – tea reached Europe in 1610, having been brought by Dutch merchants via Java. In 1664 it was introduced to England by the Portuguese wife of Charles II, Catherine of Braganza. By 1750 it was more popular than coffee.

All tea came from China until the 1830s, when the troubles there forced Britain to look elsewhere. In 1837 it was introduced to India, and to Ceylon in 1870.

That famous description of tea – 'the cup that cheers but does not inebriate' – comes from William Cowper's poem *The Task* published in 1785, and was originally written 'the cups that cheer but not inebriate'.

Tea-drinking swiftly became something of a ceremony, and in 1849 the Duchess of Bedford invented the tea-party – tiny sandwiches and cakes on a well-laid table, with a choice of Indian or China tea and a lot of gossip. Her objective, as she explained, was to fill the gap between luncheon and dinner.

The American writer Oliver Wendell Holmes summed up such occasions as: 'Giggle, gabble, gobble, git.'

T Teetotal

Teetotal   Had it not been for a Lancashire man's speech impediment – or, perhaps, his nervousness – we might now be calling non-imbibers something completely different.

Speaking out against the evils of alcohol at a meeting in 1833, a certain Joseph Turner of Preston is reported to have stammered, 'Nothing but t-t-t-t-t-total abstinence will do . . .'

Apparently seized upon in derision to start with, the stuttered expression was later adopted by the abstainers to describe their position.

> *The cook was a good cook, as cooks go; and as cooks go she went.*
> *Saki*

Temperance   The American statesman and lawyer William Maxwell Evarts, a master of the well-turned phrase, was Secretary of State when the President of the USA was Rutherford B. Hayes – a fervent advocate of temperance.

Of one diplomatic function Evarts remarked dryly, 'It was a brilliant affair; water flowed like champagne.'

Texas Rattlesnake   *First catch your rattlesnake – carefully. Skin and cut it into 3″ – 4″ pieces. Roll in a mixture of flour, cornmeal, milk and egg. Salt and pepper and deep-fry in oil. Serve HOT.*

Three Sheets in the Wind   A nautical expression meaning 'very drunk'. The sheet is the rope attached to the clew of a sail. If the sheet is quite free, the sail flaps without restraint and the sheet is said to be 'in the wind'.

A sheet in the wind is colloquial for being tipsy. So to have three sheets in the wind is to be very drunk indeed.

> *Captain Cuttle looking, candle in hand, at Bunsby, more attentively, perceived that he was three sheets in the wind, or, in plain words, drunk.*
> *Dickens: Dombey & Son*

Thyme

This strong-tasting aromatic herb – found throughout Europe, Asia and North America – has been used for culinary, medicinal and decorative purposes since ancient times.

Its name may have come from the ancient Greek word *thymon* (to fumigate), or from *thymus,* meaning 'courage', as the herb was used as a symbol of bravery.

Medicinally it has been used as tea sweetened with honey for colds, sore throats and digestive problems; the ancient Greeks used to burn it as incense in their temples.

A few thyme plants in the garden will encourage bees. The wonderful flavour of the Greek Hymettus honey comes from the wild thyme on which the bees feed.

Tipping

In the early days, waiting staff were not paid at all and it was the tips that gave them the means to live. Often, in the better restaurants, head waiters would buy their position and pay the establishment a weekly amount for the privilege of working there.

The practice of tipping seems now to have got so out of hand that it no longer signifies appreciation of good service rendered – rather something that is expected as a right, irrespective of whether it has been deserved.

To increase their profits, some places add a 'service charge' to the bill and keep it, rather than passing it on to the staff.

Fresh lemon or orange juice frozen in ice-cube trays makes an original touch when mixing drinks.

Tippler

Now used to describe the fan of more than just the occasional drink (or tipple), a tippler was originally a tavern-keepr, and his tavern was called a tippling house.

T Toasts

Toasts

The custom of lifting the glass towards the person to whose health one drinks goes back thousands of years. The ancient Greeks proposed toasts with the words 'It is to you', and then handed the cup to the individual toasted, so that he could drink from it in turn.

The word 'toast' comes from the habit of actually floating bits of toasted bread in the wine to improve its often disgusting taste. The idea was that the toast would soak up any sediment floating in the drink.

The Scandinavian word *skoll* literally means 'skull', as the ancient Vikings had the unlovely habit of making their enemies' skulls into drinking vessels.

'Here's mud in your eye' indicates that the drinker will down his drink in one go. It probably stems from the time when wine had so much sediment that it could be likened to mud – so when the drinker up-ended his glass he would literally have 'mud in his eye'.

At formal dinners and banquets it is an established custom that there is no smoking until after the loyal toast, after which the formalities can be relaxed. At some intercontinental dinners the loyal toast is drunk immediately after grace to prevent any unenlightened foreigner erring in the necessary etiquette.

Only the Royal Navy can drink the toast sitting down. Whilst serving in the Navy, William IV, a tall man, kept bumping his head on the wardroom ceiling when he rose to toast George IV. When he became monarch, he issued orders that on board ship the company could remain seated during the toast.

There are some eccentric customs associated with toasts. In the 17th century (and still at certain eccentric gatherings today) the Jacobites, when asked to drink to a monarch they thought of as a usurper, would pass their glasses over the water-filled fingerbowl. Thus they would be toasting their own exiled Stuart 'King across the water'.

The habit of hurling one's glass into the fireplace after the toast was to ensure that that glass could not be used to honour any other person.

In 18th-century society, diners were often called upon for 'sentiments' (epigrammatical observations or wishes) expressed at the end of a meal. Robert Clive (Clive of India) for example would say 'Alas and alackaday' (a lass and a lac – 100,000 rupees – a day).

Tomato Juice   Great in Bloody Marys – but beware:

> *An accident happened to my*
> *brother Jim,*
> *Somebody threw a tomato at him.*
> *Tomatoes are juicy and don't hurt*
> *the skin,*
> *But this one was specially packed in*
> *a tin.*

Tomato Ketchup   Children have found tomato ketchup a useful device for disguising the taste of everything they eat. But mix tomato sauce with mustard, Worcester sauce, cayenne, brown sugar, salt, pepper and lemon juice and you have a wonderful spicy sauce for baby sausages, barbecues etc. Tomato sauce does nothing for the flavour of fish. Remember:

> *If you do not shake the bottle,*
> *None'll come and then a lot'll.*

To Sit above the Salt   Once the family salt cellar (saler) was of silver and always put in the middle of the table. Guests of distinction were placed above the saler, nearest to the host. Inferior guests and dependents sat below.

It was a not-so-subtle way of showing who was who.

Treasure   Every home should have one. A Treasure is that member of the household who generally has the responsibility for running the kitchen. Caterers and other professionals are often told – in reverential whispers – of Treasure who would be 'only too pleased to assist'.

T **Tumbler**

In reality Treasure often turns out to be an old retainer who has to be humoured, fed and given drinks, and who becomes one more person determined to get in the way. They complain that whatever is being done is not the way it should be done in their kitchen, and that, in any event, it would have been done by them much more efficiently. Not that they wanted to, however.

It is Treasure who is greeted with whoops of delight by the guests and profusely thanked for preparing such a delicious meal and a wonderful party, and for all the hard work. An endless procession of family and friends pay court and Treasure accepts all of this as being rightfully due. When the washing-up starts, Treasure, of course, has to go.

In literature you'll often come across buried treasures. Most Treasures found in kitchens deserve to be.

To salvage curdled mayonnaise: tip into a jug, add another egg to the bowl or blender, and gradually add the curdled mixture.

Tumbler

The original 17th-century drinking glass was not flat-bottomed, but had a rounded or pointed base. It could not be put down without 'tumbling' and spilling its contents.

The drinker thus had no choice but to drain the glass before laying it down . . .

> *I look upon it, that he who does not mind his belly will hardly mind anything else.*
> Samuel Johnson

Turkey

In a Mediterranean restaurant the following was overheard:
'Waiter, what is the turkey like?'
'Like big chicken, sir.'

Turkey's the bird without which Christmas is incomplete on this side of the Atlantic, and Thanksgiving on the other. Its name, naturally, has nothing to do with that Mediterranean country.

Originally domesticated by the Aztec Indians of Mexico, the turkey was brought to Europe by Levantine merchants, and thence to England about 1540. These merchants (presumably because of their Turkish orgins) were called turkey merchants, so the birds first became 'turkey birds' and, eventually, just turkeys.

Opinions on the culinary worth of turkey flesh vary substantially. Brillat-Savarin declared that it was 'if not the most delicate, at least the most flavourful of our domestic birds'. William Connor, writing in the *Daily Mirror*, was of a different view: 'What a shocking fraud the turkey is. In life preposterous, insulting . . . in death unpalatable.'

There has always been a tendency to over-roast the turkey, pack it with a generally unpalatable breadcrumb stuffing, and serve it up with leathery roast potatoes. But it doesn't have to be like that.

With patience, or if you can find a good butcher, the bird can be boned out, stuffed with any sort of stuffing loaded with lots of herbs, grated orange, minced ham, and other goodies, sewn up into a parcel, baked in foil and served either hot or cold in large slices with a redcurrant, orange and port jelly. It cheers up the old bird no end.

Unpublished Cookbooks and Guides

Anorexia Nervosa: An Investigation by the Sumo Wrestlers' Association
Cooking with Guinness by the Board of Directors
Life without Beer by the Professional Darts Guild
Alfred the Great's 100 Best Cake Recipes
The Role of Nouvelle Cuisine in Pub Food
The Good Butcher's Guide to Vegetarian Restaurants

Veganism

An extension of vegetarianism which is strict to the point of impossibility.

Vegans give up not only meat and fish, but things like eggs and cheese as well, because they relate to living entities.

V **Vegatarianism**

An oven cleans much more easily when it is warm.

Vegetarianism Vegetarianism is the total rejection of the eating of flesh in any shape or form. It originally began in the East as a discipline for priests.

Many famous men, from George Bernard Shaw to Adolf Hitler, have been vegetarians, but in England it did not find favour until the 19th century. Before that time, vegetables were very rarely eaten.

Too many vegetarians tend to be so proud of their calling that they insist upon telling everyone else within earshot the pitfalls of not following their lead.

Many vegetarians tend to be non-drinkers as well, although why the juice of the grape should be damned in company with the flesh of the lamb is not entirely clear.

Vegetarian restaurants have a reputation for being full of fairly unkempt people eating their way slowly through what looks like a great deal of stodge. A touch unfair, maybe, but Western cultures tend not to appreciate the fine art of cooking interesting vegetarian meals. To sample the best of either Indian or Thai vegetarian cooking is almost enough to convert the most dedicated meat-eater.

A story is told of J. M. Barrie who was once seated next to George Bernard Shaw at a dinner party. Shaw, a vegetarian, had been provided with a dish of salad greens. Barrie looked at this unpleasant-looking concoction and then whispered to Shaw, 'Tell me, have you eaten that or are you going to?'

> *Omelettes are not made without breaking eggs.*
> **Robespierre**

Vermouth An essential ingredient to a proper dry Martini, the drink has Italian associations. The word 'Vermouth' is in fact derived from the old English word *wermod* – or in German *wermut* – the root of the bitter herb (wormwood) from which this drink is made.

Originally wormwood was favoured as a hermifage – for purging intestinal parasites. In the late 17th century it was promoted as an aid to the digestion and in the next century the essence of wormwood was mixed with other herbs and added to sweetened white wine.

The first vermouth to be launched commercially, in 1786, was Punt é Mes. This means 'point and a half', a popular phrase on the Stock Market near the bar where it was first sold.

Vine

The vine is mentioned in Genesis and in the oldest known Egyptian and Greek writings.

According to the *Talmud* it was Noah who planted the vine. When the devil asked him what he was doing and why, Noah explained:

'I am planting a vine. Its fruit, freshly picked or dried, is sweet and good: the pressed juice gladdens the heart of man.'

'Let us work together,' the devil said, and after the vine was planted he fetched a lamb, a lion, a monkey and a pig, cut their throats and poured their blood on the ground.

'That is why when man eats the fruit of the vine he is as gentle as a lamb; when he drinks wine he believes himself a lion; if, by chance, he drinks too much he grimaces like a monkey; and when he is often drunk he is nothing more than a vile pig.'

Today blood, either dried or natural, is still fed to vines as a nutrient to induce growth.

In cooking, as in all the arts, simplicity is the sign of perfection.
Curnonsky

Vinegar

An old French word that means 'sour wine', vinegar was discovered by the ancient Egyptians, though to them it was only beer that had gone sour.

Vinegar cuts through grease and adds piquancy to dressings and marinades; it preserves and has a stabilising effect – especially on eggs in meringues and mayonnaise.

Add a little vinegar to red vegetables and they will keep their colour while cooking. Curiously, it has the opposite effect on green vegetables.

Any leftover wine will soon turn to vinegar if the bottle-neck is covered with a cloth to let the air in. Make herb vinegar by adding herbs to the bottle and allowing them to marinate.

Vino Veritas Translated this means 'There is truth in wine', and it's a very good phrase to remember.

Alcohol loosens, amongst other things, the tongue – encouraging the imbiber to utter words that, if remembered the next day, tend to bring embarrassment and recrimination! So always make sure that the brain is in gear before the mouth is open.

The English variant of the Latin phrase, is 'When the wine is in, the wits are out'.

Vol-au-vent Rounds of puff pastry that are the mainstay of many caterers. Invariably filled with a thick white sauce which has a little fish or chicken included, vol-au-vents are always served cold.

They taste terrible.

But filled with curried smoked fish or prawns in garlic butter, and served HOT, they are transformed.

VSOP Very Special (or Superior) Old Pale is a Cognac blend which takes at least five years to mature. Not a legal definition like *appellation controlée,* its use doesn't necessarily mean one is getting the real thing. Buy with care!

Try adding a little sugar to correct an over-salty soup or casserole.

Water of Life *Eau de Vie* is brandy, and is a French translation of the Latin *aqua vitae* – 'water of life'.

Whisky is a corruption of the Gaelic *uisgebeatha* – water of life, again.

The water of life was originally sold by alchemists, and made from distilled spirits which were claimed to have the power to prolong life. Whether one can claim longevity for consistent tipplers of either brandy or whisky is open to question – but what a way to go!

Which Wine? Which wine should be drunk with which food really is a matter of personal taste. But there are a few sensible rules that should govern one's choices. They were devised to give eaters the greatest pleasure and they should not be ignored out of hand.

No point in drinking warm Spatelese with the roast beef, or '76 Claret with scampi. Both the food and the drink will suffer.

The general rules are:

● white meat – white wine; red meat – red wine
● heavy foods – heavy wine; light foods – light wine
● spicy foods – beer, or very cold white wine
● desserts – dessert (sweet) wine.

It has been said that champagne will go with everything, but in truth the best thing to accompany a bottle of champagne is a second bottle.

> **Work is the curse of the drinking classes.**
> *Oscar Wilde*

Worcester- Marcus, Lord Sandys, a former Governor of Bengal, had a liking for hot,
shire Sauce spicy foods and on his return to England in 1835 took his recipe for a hot relish to a pharmacy run by John Lea and William Perrins and asked them to make it up.

They found the result unpalatable, so stored it away in stone jars and forgot about it.

Some time later they discovered the jars again, tasted it and found it had matured into a superb sauce. They asked Lord Sandys for permission to make the sauce commercially, and first sold it in 1837.

Since then 'The Original and Genuine Lea and Perrins Worcestershire Sauce', in its distinctive livery, has travelled around the world, and remains an essential stock item in any civilised kitchen.

Whisky There are five countries currently producing drinkable whiskies – Scotland, America, Canada, Ireland and Japan.

Scottish, Canadian and Japanese bottles use the WHISKY spelling – America and Ireland spell it WHISKEY.

Scotch whisky is made both from malt and from grain, and though Irish whiskey is similarly distilled, there is a a marked difference in taste between the two. Bourbon is made only in the USA; Canada and America both make rye whiskey.

Japan produces its own malt and mixes it with bulk whisky bought from Scotland. At one stage Japanese names for whisky emulated Scottish brands, but now Japan has the fourth-largest international liquor group and produces the world's costliest whisky.

An American university professor has written that a litre of whisky drunk in five minutes before a nuclear explosion would reduce the radiation danger to the body by half.

Mind you, the alcoholic poisoning would finish you off . . .

X 'X' was marked on beer casks to indicate that excise duty had been paid and that the beer was therefore of a recognised strength. Brewers then began marking two or threes 'X's to indicate better quality, and the habit spread to all drinks.

Do not take too much notice. Cooking brandy is often marked 'XXXX', but then so is one brand of Australian beer . . .

Moderation is a fatal thing, Lady Hunstanton. Nothing succeeds like excess.
Oscar Wilde

Fine Ripe Oranges

To segment an orange perfectly, slice off the top and bottom, stand the fruit on a flat surface, and with a sharp knife slice off skin and pith all round the orange. Then cut down between segments and membrane and push up against the next membrane. Repeat with all segments.

Yogurt Legend has it that an angel handed down to Abraham the secret of making yogurt.

In the Balkans it has long been thought to promote long life – perhaps something to do with the fact that Abraham lived to be 175 and fathered a child at 100.

History tells us that Francois I, King of France when Henry VIII was on the throne of England, suffered from an obstinate stomach complaint. He summoned a Jewish doctor from Constantinople who was renowned for curing such cases. The doctor arrived with a flock of sheep and cured his royal majesty, but refused to divulge the secret of his concoctions.

It's a fair bet they were based on yogurt.

Natural live yogurt is undoubtedly a very valuable food – the sweetened, pasteurised and fruit-flavoured variety perhaps less so!

Z Zest

Yorkshire Pudding

> *Let us call Yorkshire pudding*
> *A fortunate blunder;*
> *It's a sort of popover*
> *That's tripped and popped under.*

So declared Ogden Nash, but perhaps he'd only eaten the soggy part from underneath the roast.

The light and crispy pieces from the edge of the roasting tin are delicious, and these days are no longer served as a first course to fill you up and make sure you don't eat too much meat.

Trust a thrifty Yorkshireman to think of that one!

Zabaglione

Zabaglione, or in French *sabayon,* is a very peculiar dish which could be classed either as food or drink. It is often used as a sauce poured over a dessert, but it can be eaten by itself with a great deal of enjoyment – or drunk out of the glass in which it is prepared.

The recipe consists merely of egg yolks, sugar and Marsala, served hot in small goblets or saucer champagne glasses and eaten with a spoon.

Definitely worth trying on a cold winter's day.

Zest

Zeste in French is the peel of an orange or lemon.

The word 'zest' in a recipe indicates the thinnest outer layer of that peel, with no pith.

Classically, the zest is best drawn from the peel by rubbing sugar lumps over the orange or lemon until the colour and essence are absorbed.

'Zest' is also the thing you are left without after a hard day's cooking.

> *There is no love sincerer than the*
> *love of food.*
> **George Bernard Shaw**